INSIGHT POCKET GUIDES

Bavaria

Original

GW00505047

APA PUBLICATIONS

Part of the Langenscheidt Publishing Group

Der **Marienaltar** im südlichen Seitenschiff (um 1520) stammt von einem unbekannten Meister, wahrscheinlich aus der Riemenschneiderschule. Im Schrein : Marias Krönung; in der Predella : der Tod Marias; auf den Flügeln : Anna Selbdritt und Maria mit Kind.

Auf der Westempore steht der **Heilig-Blut-Altar,** ein Meisterwerk des berühmten Würzburger Bildhauers Tilman Riemenschneider. Der Altar entstand in den Jahren 1499 bis 1505 im Auftrag des Rothenburger Rates, um der im Mittelalter verehrten Heilig-Blut-Reliquie einen neuen würdigen Rahmen zu geben. Diese wird in der Bergkristall-kapsel des Reliquienkreuzes (um 1270) über der Schreinmitte aufbewahrt. Die Abendmahlsszene darunter ist von großer Ausdruckskraft; Christus kennzeichnet den Verräter Judas. Johannes liegt an der Brust seines Herrn. Die Seitenflügel zeigen den Einzug Jesu in Jerusalem (links) und sein Gebet im Garten Gethsemane (rechts). Der Altaraufbau kommt aus der Werkstatt des Rothenburger Meisters Erhard Harschner.

Die zum Teil sehr schönen **Steinplastiken** und **Bilder** im Hauptschiff stammen größtenteils von unbekannten Meistern. Besonders bemerkenswert : An der Nordwand : Eine frühgotische Maria und ein Schmerzensmann. An der Südwand : Eine spätgotische Maria. An den Säulen : Der Heilige Christophorus, St. Georg, Johannes der Evangelist, Johannes der Täufer und ein wertvolles Marienbild von Friedrich Herlin. Vor der Empore : Der Heilige Eustachius und eine besonders schöne Bischofsfigur. Die Kanzel stammt aus der Zeit von 1854.

Die neue **Orgel** auf der Westempore wurde 1968 eingeweiht. Sie verfügt über zwei Spieltische, sechs Manuale und mehr als 5000 Pfeifen.

Diese Kirche und Ihre Kunstwerke wurden zum Lob Gottes geschaffen. Sie laden uns ein in das Psalmwort einzustimmen : „Lobe den Herrn, meine Seele, und vergiß nicht, was er dir Gutes getan hat."

Dollmann Druck GmbH · 74572 Blaufelden-Wiesenbach

Kurzführer
durch die Evang.-Luth.

St.-Jakobs-Kirche
in
Rothenburg ob der Tauber

Welcome!

Dabbling my feet in lakes, climbing mountains, hiding in pine forests – these are my memories of Bavaria as a child. The region was an intense experience of colour and sound, excitement and romance. Since then I have visited over 100 countries, and yet if anything Bavaria now seems to me even more extraordinary.

In these pages, Insight Guides' correspondent in Bavaria, Anne Midgette, distils the essential magic of the region in a series of carefully crafted itineraries. She begins in Munich, Bavaria's capital, then embarks on a roughly clockwise tour, beginning in the south with Upper Bavaria then following the Romantic Road north to Franconia and then east to Lower Bavaria. Recommended stops for rest and refreshment are included, and supporting the itineraries are sections on shopping, eating out and nightlife, plus a practical information section.

Anne Midgette lives and works as a journalist in Munich. She first came to Bavaria from the United States in 1986. Three days after her arrival, some friends loaded her into their car and whisked her off to a grassy meadow on the side of the snowcapped Alps, where people were drinking mugs of beer at long wooden tables while green-clad men with what looked like shaving brushes on their hats oom-pahed away on brass instruments. Behind them loomed the spires of Mad King Ludwig's famous Neuschwanstein. At that moment, she says, she wondered if she had left reality altogether. Since then she has come to realise that Bavaria is very much a country unto itself, where the people are fiercely proud of their unique culture.

C O N T E N T S

History & Culture

From the Romans to the Wittelsbach dynasty, from the Counter-Reformation to Hitler's bid for power in a Munich beer hall – an introduction to the forces and personalities that have shaped Bavaria's history **10–17**

Bavaria's Highlights

15 itineraries taking you to the best of Bavaria. From Munich, the book moves south to Upper Bavaria, then follows a clockwise route along the Romantic Road to Franconia, where it heads east to Lower Bavaria.

MUNICH

UPPER BAVARIA

THE ROMANTIC ROAD

Pages 2/3: a fairy-tale land

Pages 8/9:
the festive spirit

HISTORY &

Bavaria's borders have fluctuated over the centuries, but its core has remained fundamentally unchanged; the land between the river Danube and the Alps, the rivers Lech and Inn, has consistently remained the centre of a single political, sociological entity.

The first 'Bavarians' lived here about 600,000 years ago, but the Celts, who appeared between 700 and 500BC, made a far more tangible mark on the region. Their legacies include the remains of villages and religious sites as well as some blond-haired, blue-eyed genes which crop up now and then among the generally dark-complexioned locals.

In 15BC, Augustus Caesar's Roman armies marched in and conquered all of Southern Germany in a single summer. In their new province, *Rhaetium*, the ever-efficient Romans set up military encampments, many of which became urban centres that still exist today. One such is *Rhaetium's* capital *Augusta Vindelicum*, today known as Augsburg; there are other Roman remains in *Castra Regina* (Regensburg) and *Boiodurum* (Passau).

But Rome gradually overextended itself until Imperial troops could no longer withstand the onslaughts of Germanic tribes – at home or abroad. In AD476, Odoacer, leader of Germanic troops within the Roman armies, overthrew the Roman Emperor, establishing an Ostrogoth Empire and ending the Roman Empire for good.

Mask of a Roman soldier

Culture

Early Christians and Medieval Dukes

When the Romans were gone, so popular legend has it, the *Baiuvarii* tribe returned to the lands from which they'd been expelled. During the reign of the Agilolfing family in the 7th century, Irish monks zealously embarked on missionary work. Saints and martyrs Magnus, Boniface, and Kilian were among those who spread the Catholic gospels and established bishoprics, churches and monasteries (the Marienkapelle in Würzburg, St Emmeram in Regensburg, and Benedictine monasteries on Lake Chiemsee).

Selling spices

In 788, Charlemagne decided that Duke Tassilo III of the Agilofing family was getting too big for his britches, deposed him, and absorbed his territories into the Carolingian Empire. The Carolingian dynasty died out, however, in 911, and control of the region was hotly disputed over the next two centuries. Significant among the six dynasties who held power during this period were the Welfs, whose rule saw the growth of a little river community called Munichen (München, or Munich); but Emperor Frederick I Barbarossa, tired of their frequent bids for more power, got rid of them in 1180, awarding the duchy to Otto I of the house of Wittelsbach. It was an auspicious move: the Wittelsbachs ruled in Bavaria as Dukes, Electors, and finally Kings, for 738 years.

The first Wittelsbach rulers devoted themselves to the pursuit of new territory, and were so successful that they were among the Holy Roman Empire's most important ruling dynasties by the middle of the 13th century. Arguments over succession, however, divided the duchy and undermined its power. The one truly strong ruler during the 14th and 15th centuries was Ludwig the Bavarian (who had himself crowned Emperor in 1327), but the power and land gain

Jakob Fugger's office

he achieved was rapidly forgotten in territorial disputes between his six sons after his death.

Fortunately, political turmoil did not affect the art and architecture of the period. Romanesque churches made way for the soaring Gothic cathedrals of Regensburg, Munich, Landshut and Rothenburg. On the literary front, the *Nibelung* epic was completed in Passau around 1200, while, in Landshut, Wolfram von Eschenbach was finishing his poem *Parzifal* (both works later became the basis for operas by the 19th-century composer Richard Wagner). And the political insignificance of Bavaria's ruling families was balanced by the increasing power of private citizens such as the Fuggers of Augsburg, whose patriarch Jakob used his fortune to influence Imperial elections in 1519. Most Bavarians, however, lived as farmers in the countryside. Apart from the profitable salt trade there was little industry.

Bavaria Reunited

Duke Albrecht IV was tired of seeing Bavaria subdivided – and he didn't want to share the task of governing with his brother. In 1506, he established the principle of primogeniture, whereby only firstborn sons should govern; Bavaria remained under the control of one ruler until the end of the Wittelsbach era.

It was the dawn of the Renaissance. Tilman Riemenschneider and Veit Stoss were carving magnificent altars and figures for churches throughout Bavaria; Riemenschneider even had the temerity to enter politics, becoming Mayor of Würzburg in 1520. Equal skill was shown by Bavarian painters Lucas Cranach, Hans Holbein father and son, and Nuremberg native Albrecht Dürer, whose self-portraits were not only some of the finest of the Renaissance, but some of the first.

Martin Luther, meanwhile, was making waves with radical clerical reforms which split Europe into two bitterly warring factions, Catholic and Protestant. Although a German, Luther found little support in Catholic Bavaria; leaders such as Wilhelm the Pious ensured that most of the state remained a centre for the Counter-Reformation. Some neighbouring, at that

Wood-carving by Veit Stoss

time non-Bavarian cities such as Nuremberg and Regensburg did, however, vote to become Protestant, and even Augsburg developed a strong Protestant tradition.

When Duke Maximilian I took power in 1597, Bavaria was riddled with debt after the rules of two spendthrift dukes. Maximilian, however, was equal to the challenge; a born leader who was famously industrious (starting work each morning before 5am), he brought the state's account books solidly into the black within 12 years. He didn't only prove his mettle on the home front: founder of the defensive Catholic League in 1609, he led its troops to victory in the Thirty Years' War. His success was crowned when the grateful Emperor elevated him from Duke to Elector (*Kurfürst*) in

1623. Ironically, this war, which hit Bavaria hard (900 cities and towns were destroyed, and half the population lost), also helped to establish the state's importance on the European political scene. Maximilian ruled throughout the war; he died in 1651.

The physical devastation of the Thirty Years' War did have some positive consequences: people began building like mad to replace what had been lost. As new churches, palaces and administrative buildings sprang up, so did a style which was to become a hallmark of the region: Bavarian baroque. Imported from Italy by Elector Ferdinand Maria's Turin-born wife Henriette Adelaide in 1663 when she commissioned the Theatiner Church in Munich, the new style spread like wildfire, soon producing German

Maximilian I

artists able to equal, even surpass, their Italian models. Among these were the Asam brothers, Egid Quirin and Cosmas Damian, and Balthasar Neumann, who designed the Würzburg Residenz. And the word *barockisiert*, 'baroque-ised', was added to the German vocabulary as old buildings throughout Bavaria were redone in the new fashion.

Leaders and Ladies

In the late 1700s, Bavaria's political scene was dominated by one of the country's most ingenious politicians: Elector Max IV Joseph's Foreign Minister, Count Montgelas. Forced to choose between France and Austria as Europe prepared itself for yet another war, both Elector and Minister opted for France and Napoleon, signing a treaty of alliance in 1805. The decision was opportune: Napoleon promptly trounced Austria and rewarded Bavaria's loyalty with large land grants (including Augsburg and Passau) and the official title of Kingdom.

Francophilia, however, waned soon enough; in 1813, the pragmatic Bavarians switched sides. Their new treaty with Austria placed them on the side of the victorious powers at the 1815 Congress of Vienna after Napoleon's final defeat. At the Congress, new territorial grants gave Bavaria approximately the shape it has today.

Bavaria's next ruler was King Ludwig I, who filled Munich with new museums and cultural institutions, like the Alte and Neue Pinakothek, designed by royal favourite Leo von Klenze. Besides architecture, Ludwig's consuming passion was women: a series of portraits he commissioned of the kingdom's 'most beautiful women' fills an entire room in Nymphenburg Palace. This weakness for the ladies brought about the King's downfall. When 'Spanish' dancer Lola Montez (actually an Irishwoman from Limerick) performed in the National Theatre, King Ludwig was immediately smitten. His blatant attachment fuelled rising animosity among the population; ultimately, a revolution in the stormy year of 1848 forced Ludwig to abdicate in favour of his son, Maximilian II.

Dreams and Reality

In 1864, Maximilian's death cleared the throne for one of the most fantastic characters in Bavaria's history: his son, King Ludwig II. The young king, a daydreamer and passionate builder, spent all of the kingdom's money constructing castles which seemed as anachronous and even bizarre to his contemporaries as they do today, such as the famous Neuschwanstein. Politically, the most significant act of Ludwig's reign was Bavaria's entry into the new, Prussian-led German Empire, proclaimed in 1871. For the first time in centuries, Bavaria was in a submissive position among German states.

The young Ludwig II

Ludwig's eccentric behaviour became more and more pronounced, and in 1886, he was officially diagnosed as insane. A week later, he was found with his doctor, drowned; one of the region's favourite unsolved mysteries is the question of whether it was suicide or murder. Although his extravagant building projects bled his country's coffers dry, 'Mad' King Ludwig remained fixed in the popular imagination, and to this day his portrait graces shops and homes throughout Bavaria.

As Ludwig's brother Otto was even crazier than his sibling, 65-

Kurt Eisner proclaimed Bavaria a Republic

year-old Uncle Luitpold stepped in as Prince Regent, ruling until his death at the grand old age of 91. After the flighty control of Ludwig II, who had been happy to leave the work of governing to his ministers, Luitpold brought dignity back to the monarchy without undermining the power of the parliaments, and returned prosperity to the land. After Luitpold's death, his son put an end to the regency and ascended the throne as King Ludwig III.

When the German Empire declared a state of war in 1914, Bavaria had little choice but to go along with it – and little inclination to do anything else. With the rest of the German states, the region mobilised and sent troops out to fight the bloody battles of World War I. As German losses mounted, however, unrest began at home, leading, in Bavaria, to revolution. In 1918, socialist leader Kurt Eisner proclaimed Bavaria a Free People's Republic, and announced that Wittelsbach rule was at an end. The ensuing tumultuous months saw the assassination of Eisner, the establishment of a soviet republic, or *Räterepublik*, and its violent overthrow at the hands of the conservative White Guard.

The storm died down when the 'Bamberg Constitution' officially termed Bavaria a 'Free State and Member of the German Empire'; but this did nothing to solve unemployment and inflation so extreme that it took an entire wheelbarrow full of money to buy a loaf of bread. Suffering from privation and angry at ineffective leadership, the people were looking for a saviour; and they saw him in an Austrian named Adolf Hitler. Although Hitler's first bid for power in a Munich beer hall in 1923 was put down, his National Socialist party continued to gain ground; in 1933, he was named Chancellor and the Third Reich had begun.

Hitler was indeed able to bolster the economy; but he also dreamed of restoring to Germany the boundaries of the Holy Roman Empire, while clearing it of 'undesirables' such as Jews and homosexuals, whom he exterminated in concentration camps. 1939 saw the invasion of Poland, the beginning of the Nazi march across Europe. When the tide began to turn in the Allies' favour, retribution came in the form of massive bombings of virtually every major German city. In 1945, following the Nazi defeat, cities such as Munich, Würzburg, Augsburg and Nuremberg were in effect levelled, with only fragments of walls rising from the rubble.

Resistance leaders Hans and Sophie Scholl

Germany's rehabilitation in the eyes of the world has proceeded at varying speeds. The 1950s 'economic miracle' (*Wirtschaftswunder*), when the country was rebuilt and became prosperous in the space of a decade, won grudging admiration; some of the emotion aroused by human-rights atrocities has remained.

In 1948, Bavaria made headlines by rejecting the terms of the new German Constitution. Although the constitution was ratified, Bavaria was able to retain its title of 'Free State', as well as certain other unique privileges. Since then, the state has continued to dance to the beat of a different drummer – namely, for many years, Franz-Josef Strauss, who led Bavaria's own right-wing political party, the CSU, until his death in 1988. Conservative or no, Bavaria has prospered. After the war, many companies relocated from East Germany or no-longer-central Berlin to Bavaria, helping to build the state into a centre for science, commerce, industry, and the media.

For all of its 'otherness', it's hard to characterise 'Bavaria' as a whole. Today's state represents one-fifth of the total land mass of Germany. Within this huge area are a wealth of contrasts, of landscapes, moods, flavours.

The BMW office building in Muni

'Bavaria' is everything from the rural isolation of farming communities in the Bavarian Forest to the medieval perfection of a city like Bamberg; from the tradition of its folk customs to the high-tech of companies like BMW (Bavarian Motor Works).

Perhaps no outsider like myself will ever quite be able to take for granted things which, to Bavarians, seem perfectly normal: the elaborate wall paintings on the houses of Alpine villages, or city streets which have remained basically unchanged since 1500. Yet Bavaria, for all of these 'fairy-tale' elements, is very real indeed. Most of its old cities and historic buildings are the backdrop to an active, modern daily life; few have become museum pieces for tourists. The past is a part of life here, to be lived with and built on. Even after the destruction caused by World War II Bavaria picked itself up out of the rubble and rebuilt its cities, complete with monuments old and new dedicated to distant glories and the promise not to repeat more recent nightmares. And life goes on.

Historical Highlights

500,000–700,000BC First people in Bavaria.

700–500BC Advent of Celts.

15BC Romans conquer the region in a single summer.

AD402 Start of Roman pull-out.

493 Theodoric establishes the Ostrogoth Empire.

788 Tassilo III, the last of the Agilolfing Dukes, is deposed by Charlemagne, and Bavaria is incorporated into the Carolingian Empire.

817 The Empire is partitioned, and Bavaria is placed under the control of 13-year-old King Ludwig 'the German'.

1156 The duchy of Bavaria is separated from the rest of the *Ostmark* (Eastern Marches of the Empire).

1180 Frederick I Barbarossa awards Bavaria to Otto I of the Wittelsbach family.

1214 The Upper Palatinate (*Oberpfalz*) is awarded to Bavaria.

1506 Splintered through being divided among ducal descendants, Bavaria is reunited when the law of primogeniture passed by Duke Albrecht IV empowers only first-born sons to rule.

1623 Bavaria becomes an Electorate under Maximilian I.

1648 End of the Thirty Years' War.

1803 'Secularisation': 131 monasteries are dissolved and many are destroyed.

1805 Bavarian Foreign Minister Montgelas signs treaty with Napoleon.

1806 Bavaria becomes a Kingdom; Elector Max IV Joseph becomes King Max I.

1808 Montgelas writes first Bavarian constitution.

1818 Constitution revised; two-chamber parliament implemented.

1848 Abdication of Ludwig I.

1871 German Empire proclaimed: Bavaria is a member state, but Prussia leads.

1886 'Mad' King Ludwig II drowns mysteriously in Lake Starnberg.

1914 Declaration of war; start of World War I.

1918 King Ludwig III abdicates, ending 738 years of Wittelsbach rule.

1919 Murder of Socialist leader Kurt Eisner; short-lived soviet Republic of Bavaria. Parliamentary democracy begins.

1920 The city of Coburg votes itself into Bavaria.

1923 With the 'Beer Hall Putsch', the Nazis under Adolf Hitler try unsuccessfully to overthrow of the Bavarian government.

1933 Bavaria loses state autonomy.

1938 Synagogues and Jewish businesses attacked and ravaged. Austria and Czech Sudetenland annexed to Germany.

1939 The German invasion of Poland leading to the outbreak of World War II.

1940–45 Nazi massacre of German Jews. Munich, Nuremberg, Würzburg, Augsburg, and other cities devastated in Allied bombing raids.

1943 The *Weisse Rose*, the anti-Nazi resistance movement at Munich University fails, and the leaders Hans and Sophie Scholl are executed.

1945 Germany capitulates.

1948 German Constitution drawn up at Herrenchiemsee.

1949 Bavaria rejects the German Federal Republic's Constitution; as two-thirds of member states ratify it, it passes anyway.

1972 Munich hosts the Olympic Games.

1988 Death of Franz-Josef Strauss.

1989 The Berlin Wall falls, paving the way for German reunification.

1992 The new Munich airport opens. In December in Munich the first *Lichterkette* (candle vigils) protesting against violence to foreigners and minorities. 400,000 people take part.

Bavaria is quite simply a huge place. Over the years, the historic centre of the state – the provinces of Upper and Lower Bavaria and Upper Palatinate – has been enlarged by the addition of Franconia and part of Swabia. Today's Bavaria covers an area of 70,554 sq km (27,238 sq miles) – one-fifth of Germany's total land mass.

To enable the visitor to get the most out of a short trip, I have selected four key areas within the seven Bavarian provinces. In each area, I've designed day-long itineraries which include the best views of Bavaria's landscapes as well as visits to the region's beautiful old cities. For most rural routes you will need a car; city itineraries can all be accessed by train.

With Munich, the Bavarian capital, as the point of departure, the first of the four key areas covered by the itineraries is the province most visitors equate with 'Bavaria': **Upper Bavaria** (*Oberbayern*), including the Alps and King Ludwig's castles. To the west is the **Romantic Road** (*Romantische Strasse*), so called because of the incredibly romantic qualities of the well-preserved medieval towns through which it passes on its way to Würzburg in **Franconia**. The sights of this province also include the Gothic splendours of Bamberg as well as the striking rock formations of its own 'Little Switzerland' (*Fränkische Schweiz*). The last itineraries focus on rustic **Lower Bavaria** (*Niederbayern*), with the rolling woods and green vistas of the Bavarian Forest (*Bayerischer Wald*).

To follow all of these itineraries takes about two weeks and involves a lot of driving. Ideally, however, the book also enables you to select your options. No matter where you choose, Bavaria is a region for all tastes and interests.

A Bavarian landscape

1. The Bavarian Capital

A day of sightseeing in the Bavarian capital: from the Electoral Residence to Marienplatz at the city centre via the city's art museums to the 'bohemian' neighbourhood of Schwabing and the English Garden.

'World City with Heart' (*Weltstadt mit Herz*) is one slogan often used to describe Munich; 'village of millions' (*Millionendorf*) is another. The real city lies somewhere between these two extremes of a cosmopolitan urban centre and a welcoming, relaxed small town. Dating back to the 1100s, when a monastery was established on the salt route from Italy and Austria, the city has retained its old-fashioned charm while keeping pace with international trends in business, art and fashion.

The Theatinerkirche

Start your tour of Munich at the open square of **Odeonsplatz**, where the main boulevard of Ludwigstrasse runs into the downtown pedestrian zone. Before you stand the arches of the neoclassical **Feldherrnhalle**, modelled on a loggia in Florence, where Hitler marched with his followers in an unsuccessful bid for power in 1923. To your left is the entrance to

21

Outside the Cuvilliés Theatre

the formal 17th-century **Hofgarten** (Court Garden); on your right, the yellow facade of the first piece of Bavarian baroque: St Cajetan, better known as **Theatiner-kirche**. The latter wasn't the work of Bavarians, however; the Elector's Italian wife Henriette Adelaide, who commissioned the church from Italian builders in 1633, averred that the Bavarians were 'too idiotic' to undertake such a project.

Walk down Residenzstrasse to your left, past the **Residenz** (Electoral Residence). The reigning Wittelsbach family began construction on this site in 1385; successive generations made alterations to suit their needs and reflect their glory. As a result, the building – which houses several museums – is so large that it would take a day to see it in its entirety. I suggest you limit your tour to the marvellous **Cuvilliés Theatre**, a red-and-gold baroque extravaganza, and the **Antiquarium**, an impressive, 69-metre-long (226-ft) Renaissance room which spendthrift Duke Albrecht V built in 1571 to house the Electoral Library. The same Duke founded the **Schatzkammer** (Treasury), today containing a vast and valuable collection which is also worth a visit. The Residence's south facade, modelled on Florence's Pitti Palace, was built by architect Leo von Klenze for Ludwig I in 1835; Klenze was also responsible for rebuilding the nearby **National Theatre**, Munich's opera house, when the five-year-old building burnt to the ground in 1823 (the building you see today is a postwar reconstruction).

Continue along Residenzstrasse as it merges with part of the **Fußgängerzone** (pedestrian precinct) leading to central **Marien-platz**. Here, amid fountains and flowers, shoppers push past tourists waiting for the famous **Glockenspiel**, a mechanical clock whose carved figures dance and even joust (daily at 11am and 9pm, in summer also at noon and 5pm) in their niches on the ornate neo-Gothic facade of the **Neues Rathaus** (New Town Hall), which wasn't actually completed until 1908. The gilded **Madonna** in the square was erected in 1638 by Duke Maximilian I in thanks that Munich was spared in the Thirty Years' War and gives the square its name (Marienplatz = Mary's Square).

Behind one corner of the square, **St Peter's Church**, the oldest in Munich, contains art treasures and a tower with a magnificent view of the city and surroundings. You can also get a bird's-eye view from the sixth-floor **Café Glockenspiel** (entrance to its lift is around the corner on Rosenstrasse), where I suggest you have coffee and cake at eye level with the mechanical clock.

After coffee, go down Rosenstrasse which leads south to the consumer paradise of Sendlingerstrasse; a few minutes' stroll will bring you to the church of St Johannes of Nepomuk, better known as the **Asamkirche**. A tiny space crammed with sculptures and gold leaf, this 1735 church is one of the more lavish, not to say startling, works of baroque artists Egid Quirin and Cosmas Damian Asam. Whether you find it marvellous or in poor taste, it's definitely worth a look.

Go back up Sendlingerstrasse and turn right to get to Oberanger. On the other side of the street is the eclectic **Stadtmuseum** (Munich City Museum, Tuesday to Sunday 10am–5pm, Wednesday until 8.30pm), whose exhibitions range from modern painting to city history (including the wooden Morris dancers carved in the 15th century to ornament the Old Town Hall). Left on Oberanger and right on Rosental, you come to **Viktualienmarkt**, a farmer's market selling everything from Italian salami to French cheeses, while locals clad in folk costume quaff beer and eat *Wurst* at outdoor tables.

Walking up the street by the market brings you to bustling **Tal** where you can stop for lunch at the **Weisses Bräuhaus** (im Tal 7, tel: 089-299875), serving cuisine that's as authentically Bavarian as the surroundings. True Münchners come here at 11am to eat *Weisswurst*, a speciality of the city.

If you go up Sparkassenstrasse, a right turn followed by a left will bring you to the famous **Hofbräuhaus**, offering similar food and ambience on a larger scale, but catering more to a tourist crowd.

Artiste in the pedestrian precinct

Strolling back through Marienplatz after lunch, note the distinctive twin towers of the **Frauenkirche** (Church of Our Lady) towering behind the buildings lining the pedestrian precinct of Kaufingerstrasse. When the towers were still roofless 30 years after the church's consecration in 1495, these unique round domes were erected as a temporary solution, and became so popular that they were retained. Also of interest is the Renaissance interior of **St Michael's**, a Jesuit building from the late 16th century, on your right as you walk along the precinct. In summer, the street is crowded not only with shoppers, but also with performers, including a variety of mime artists and itinerant musicians. Ahead of you, the arch of **Karlstor**, a reconstruction of a gate in the former city walls, frames the white spume of the fountain, surrounded by people cooling their heels.

Turn to the right and walk along busy Sonnenstrasse until you can cross over to the tram stop to board tram number 27 (direction Petuelring). Travelling slowly through the heart of the city, trams are a great way to see Munich. When you see the dark stone obelisk at the centre of Karolinenplatz, get off the tram and go along Briennerstrasse toward the monumental archway looming up ahead of you at the end of **Königsplatz**.

Exhibits in the Glyptothek

Originally the work of architect von Klenze (who was kept busy by the commissions of King Ludwig I), this square saw a less glorious period when it was paved and used as a parade ground by the Nazis in the 1930s. Today, it's been restored to its original grassy self, remaining a monument to Classicism in all its forms. In addition to the arch, called the **Propyläen**, there's the **Antikensammlung**, a collection of vases and other antiquities, and the **Glyptothek** (Tuesday to Sunday 10am–5pm; Thursday until 8pm), one of my favourites, a beautiful, not-too-large museum with a fine collection of sculptures from ancient Greece and Rome.

Beyond the Propyläen, turn right up Luisenstrasse; almost immediately, you'll come upon the entrance to painter Franz von Lenbach's elegant villa, now the museum **Lenbachhaus** (Tuesday to Sunday 10am–6pm). As well as 19th-century German painting and modern exhibits, the museum is best known for its remarkable collection of works of the *Blaue Reiter* ('Blue Rider') school, a group of Munich-based artists active in the first decades of this century, including Wassily Kandinsky and Franz Marc. An underground annex in the nearby subway station, called the **Kunstbau**, displays temporary exhibitions, from African masks to contemporary art.

Munich's two main art museums can be found up Luisenstrasse and right on Theresienstrasse. The **Alte Pinakothek** (reopened, after ex-

In the beer garden

tensive renovations, in August 1998), is yet another Leo von Klenze edifice housing the magnificent painting collection of the Wittelsbach family, Old Master works with an emphasis on Dutch and Flemish schools (its collection of Rubens paintings is perhaps the finest in the world). The **Neue Pinakothek** (Tuesday to Sunday 10am– 5pm, Tuesday and Thursday until 8pm), across the street, concentrates on 19th-century European painting. It also contains a pleasant café with outdoor tables, where you can stop for *Kaffee und Kuchen* (coffee and cake).

When you've caught your breath, go two blocks up Barerstrasse to **Schellingstrasse**. This narrow street near the university is the heart of the student district, lined with funky shops and cafés. At tall Ludwigskirche, Schelling runs into Ludwigstrasse; turning left, you'll come to Geschwister-Scholl-Platz with the twin fountains before the University. From here, Veterinärstrasse leads right to the **English Garden**. Laid out in 1792, this huge public park contains everything from covered bridges to nude sunbathers, and, on sunny days, most of the population of Munich. Within the park, the pagoda of the **Chinesischer Turm** (Chinese Tower) marks the city's most famous beer garden for your evening's refreshment. If the weather's not inviting, walk up Ludwigstrasse past the **Siegestor** (Triumphal Arch) where it becomes **Leopoldstrasse**, the main artery through bohemian **Schwabing**, with plenty of sidewalk cafés, restaurants, bars and discos where you can while away the night.

If you decide you want to stay another day in Munich you might want to visit the magnificent Nymphenburg Palace to the west of the city and the futuristic Olympic Park to the north, created for the 1972 Olympic Games. Located on an island in the Isar near the city centre is the **Deutsches Museum**, a marvellous museum of science and technology. Another notable museum is the **Haus der Kunst** on Prinzregenstrasse, a venue for major travelling shows.

The English Garden

Upper Bavaria

Mountains over Mittenwald

Nowhere is Bavaria more picturesque than in the region of Upper Bavaria, its villages bright with paintings and flowers, its inhabitants dressed in the quaint local costumes of their forbears, its lakes reflecting the splendour of the surrounding mountains. Every one of these villages, furthermore, is the starting point of well-marked walking trails, from easy to arduous, which afford yet another perspective on the region, as well as a breath of the invigorating mountain air. The itineraries that follow are intended to reveal the best of Upper Bavaria, including such key destinations as Neuschwanstein Castle, Oberammergau, Garmisch, Mittenwald; Bavaria's best-known lake, Chiemsee; and the resort town of Berchtesgaden. Travellers should ideally have their own transport, but access to the key sights of each itinerary is also possible by public transport.

2. Füssen and the Royal Castles

Mad King Ludwig's medieval fantasy, the turreted castle of Neuschwanstein, and nearby Hohenschwangau, where he grew up; on to the town of Füssen, with its own old castle, medieval monastery, and charming Altstadt beside the blue river Lech.

From Munich, Füssen and Ludwig's castles are best reached by taking the *Autobahn* to Starnberg, the B2 to Weilheim, and from there the B472 to the B17, the southern section of the route called the *Romantische Strasse* (Romantic Road, *see p 42*). Having arrived in the hill resort of **Steingaden**, turn left out of the village and after about 3km (2 miles) go right down a narrow road (signposted 'Wies') to the **Wieskirche**, considered to be one of the finest examples of Bavarian baroque. Built to house a miraculous image of Mary whose eyes shed real tears, the little church standing innocuously in its meadow was the work of the great baroque artist Johann Baptist Zimmermann, and is today a site of pilgrimage for art lovers as well as worshippers.

Cherub in the Wieskirche

Return to Steingaden and continue along the B17. As the Alps loom ever nearer on the horizon (weather permitting), watch for roads to the left marked *Königsschlößer* (King's Castles). The castles in question will be visible as soon as you turn off, rising from their wooded slopes. Lower, and to the right, is yellow Hohenschwangau; on the left is the higher, grey, soaring shape familiar from picture postcards and Walt Disney logos: **Neuschwanstein**. No matter how often you've seen it, 'mad' King Ludwig II's fairy-tale castle never loses its unreal, other-worldly air. Perhaps this is because it never was quite 'real': an anachronism when it was built from 1869–86 (and never finished), the castle was only inhabited for a matter of days, and therefore its only tangible function for its entire existence has been that of a glorified stage set.

After the dramatic promise of its exterior, a tour of Neuschwanstein's interior is likely to be disappointing. Although horse-drawn carriages are available to spare you the steep, 25-minute ascent on foot from the car park in Hohenschwangau, there's no way to avoid the lines of tourists, which in the summer months often reach through the gate.

Neuschwanstein in the mist

Hohenschwangau Castle

Unless you're a real castle fan, avoid the crowded heights alto-gether, and head instead to a castle which really was inhabited, and still is: **Hohenschwangau**, on the other side of the valley. The ascent doesn't take more than five minutes; guided tours are given 8.30am–5.30pm (November to March 10.30am–4.30pm). Ludwig spent much of his youth in this castle, built as a summer palace by his father between 1835 and 1855. Inside, it preserves relics of the historical past ranging from cannonballs to one of composer Richard Wagner's pianos.

The Alpenstrasse leads to **Füssen**, 4km (2½ miles) away. Dating back to Roman times, later reclaimed by the Irish monks who ar-rived in Bavaria spreading Catholicism in the 8th and 9th century, this historic old town is in my opinion every bit as interesting to visit as the more famous castles nearby. In fact, it has its own me-dieval castle perched above the town, as well as the monastery founded by the Irish monk Magnus, St Mang in local parlance, on the banks of the river Lech. The ascent to the **castle**, former Residence of the Prince-Bishops of Augsburg, is worthwhile for a look at its Gothic courtyard, the only one in Germany, with its unique *trompe l'oeil* paint-ing. At the foot of its hill stands the **monastery church**, a lovely piece of baroque free of some of the excesses of other contemporary buildings.

Winter near Füssen

Part of the monastery now serves as the **Rathaus** (Town Hall); off its main courtyard, you'll also find the interesting **City Museum** (*Museum der Stadt Füssen*; open April to October 11am–4pm, November to March 2pm–4pm, closed Monday). In addition to relics of the monks from Romanesque to baroque times and the **St Anna** chapel with its striking Dance of Death (*Totentanz*) frescoes, the museum highlights the local craft of lute-making. In the Renaissance, Füssen was Germany's leading centre for this trade; as its strict, 12-member guild had no room for newcomers, apprentices who completed their training were forced to go elsewhere; many went south to Italy, where their skills flourished. From the lute was born such stringed instruments as the violin; Italian violin makers, some say, have Füssen to thank for the emergence of their craft.

As you walk toward the river from the Rathaus, you can see three crosses at the top of the mountain above you: the summit of an elaborate **Stations of the Cross**. Cross the river Lech and turn right; 200m (650ft) along to the left, the little **Church of our Lady** was the site where plague victims, who had to be buried out of town, were interred. Here begins the way up the mountain, past 12 little houses decorated by painters of the Nazarene school, a group of artists formed around 1810 who worked in a style inspired by the paintings of the Middle Ages. The summit presents a superb panoramic view of the town and, in the other direction, Ludwig's castles.

For the return route, follow paths to **Lechfall** – and even if you're not up to the 1½-hour hike up to the summit and back, make sure you don't miss the sight of this broad, white waterfall thundering from the azure-blue Lech river. You can also witness the spectacle by simply continuing along Tirolerstrasse past the plague church.

Relaxing at Albsee

If you're not in a hurry to go back to Munich or have arranged to stay in Füssen (see *Accommodation* in *Practical Information, page 82*), return along the Lech to the cobbled streets of the Old Town and adjourn for dinner in the restaurant **Zum Schwanen**, housed in a 15th-century building (Brotmarkt 4, tel: 08362-6174), or the more modest but tasteful **Tiroler Weinstube**, which is upstairs at Franziskanergasse 1 (tel: 08362-6259).

From the murals and flowers on the house fronts of Oberammergau via Linderhof, King Ludwig's favourite castle, to Lake Eibsee at the foot of Germany's highest mountain, the Zugspitze, with its magnificent views.

'I thought I was in Disneyland,' said an American friend of his first sight of **Oberammergau**; and indeed, this little village seems almost too pretty to be real. Reached by taking the Garmisch *Autobahn* from Munich, then turning right after Oberau onto the B23 (1–1½ hours' drive altogether), Oberammergau is overshadowed by grey, rocky peaks, surrounded by green meadows, with its typical painted houses alternating with brown barns where cows quietly chew

Facade with 'Lüftlmalerei'

their cud. Inhaling deeply (preferably at a safe distance from the cows), you can understand why the cool, bracing air of the mountains is said to have healing properties, and why Oberammergau, like so many other villages in the Alps, is an official health resort (*Luftkurort*) where people come not, as in other fashionable resorts, to give themselves airs, but to take them.

As you walk through the streets of the town, take special note of the house facades. The art of *Lüftlmalerei* (airy painting), the facade frescoes of historical or religious subjects seen in so many Bavarian towns, originated in Oberammergau. Although houses were painted before his day, Franz Zwinck (1748–92) boosted the custom from quaint tradition to a recognised form of folk art.

Walking up Dorfstrasse from the church, turn left onto Verlegergasse toward the **Pilatus House**, a major work of Zwinck's from 1784, restored in 1909. Today, the lavishly decorated house contains a shop, and, in summer, a workshop where various artisans – wood-cutters, jewellers, and the like – practice their trade.

Leaving the Pilatus House, follow Steinbachergasse over Dorfstrasse to the **Passionsspielhaus** (Playhouse) where, every ten years, the town's famous Passion Play is performed. The 6-hour retelling of the life and passion of Christ, cast with local villagers, is staged as the result of a vow made in 1633: the plague had struck, and the townspeople pledged to perform the play if the Lord would spare their village from annihilation. The next performance will take place in 2000; until then, permanent exhibits about the play are on display at the playhouse (10.30am–12pm and 1.30pm–4.30pm, closed Monday and November 20 to December 20).

A local craft

If it wasn't already clear from numerous shops you passed on your way through town, sculptures for sale in the theatre lobby will make you aware of the fact that Oberammergau is also a centre for the regional craft of wood-carving. Before retracing your route on the B23, look in on the little rococo **church of SS Peter and Paul** on Pfarrplatz.

After about 3km (2 miles), take the right-hand turnoff to Graswang and Linderhof, and drive 9km (5 miles) through the tranquil valley to **Linderhof Castle** (open year-round, during summer 9am–5.30pm; October to March 10am–4pm; closed 12.15–12.45pm. Grotto closed in winter). The best of King Ludwig's castles – and the only one he actually lived in – Linderhof, built between 1870 and 1877, was inspired by French models, a sharp contrast to the German heritage of Neuschwanstein. Surrounded by fountains and a formal French garden, it includes such features as an underground grotto, complete with fake 'stalactites' and a lake, where the eccentric king was fond of being rowed about in a boat among the swans as he watched private performances of Wagner operas.

From Linderhof, go back towards the B23; before Graswang, on the left, is the steep uphill driveway of the restaurant **Gröbl-Alm** (Tel: 08822-6434), where you can eat a hearty Bavarian lunch looking down over the green valley and the Alps.

As you drive back towards the B23, you're following the route taken by Ludwig the Bavarian in 1330. Returning from the trip to Rome on which he was crowned Holy Roman Emperor with something less than unanimous approval, Ludwig was riding through this valley when his horse fell to its knees; taking this a sign from Heaven, the Emperor vowed to found a Benedictine monastery on the site. The result, **Kloster Ettal**, lies 1km east of the junction on the B23. If you want to look in at the round domed church, 'baroque-ised' in the mid-18th century, you can pick up a few bottles of Ettal beer as a souvenir; the monastery is one of the few in Bavaria which has managed to preserve its traditional brewery and distillery.

As you drive south towards **Garmisch** on the B23, you may no-

Linderhof Castle gardens

tice a paraglider or two spiralling earthward from the mountain heights. One of the central resorts in the Alps and host to the 1936 Winter Olympics – the ski jump and stadium are still in evidence – Garmisch is a prime destination for sportsmen of all descriptions, including paragliders, walkers, ice-skaters and skiers (who flock to the Zugspitzplatt, Germany's only skiable glacier). Testimony to the American army's long-time presence in the town are the McDonald's, Pizza Hut, and comfortable English-language cinema on the main street, looking somewhat incongruous among houses sporting *Lüftlmalerei* epigrams and murals.

Once you've seen the town, signs to Grainau/Eibsee will direct you to the right, through part of central Garmisch and on out toward jagged grey Alps which seem to rise directly from the valley floor. Left through **Grainau**, the road leads 10km (6 miles) through pastures and meadows to little **Eibsee**, a lake tucked in amongst the pines at the foot of Germany's tallest mountain, the **Zugspitze**. By the lake is the station for the cable car (*Eibsee-Seilbahn*); if you've a head for heights, buy a return ticket and board one of the bright red cars, looking like childrens' toys, which leave every half-hour for the 10-minute ascent high over the craggy slopes to the summit. At 2,964m (9,724ft), the Zugspitze is neatly divided by the Austrian border, but Germany still has claim to at least half of it. From the station at the top, it's a short walk to the cross at the peak (*Spitze*) and the highest view in all of Germany.

The summit of the Zugspitze

At the foot of the mountain, on the lake, the **Eibsee Hotel** (tel: 08821-98810), which was once patronised by the likes of Thomas Mann and other artistic and literary figures seeking a weekend's respite from Munich, has maintained its charm, even if its prices have risen over the years. The restaurant, its lakeside balcony commanding a marvellous view of the Zugspitze, offers fine dining for a pretty penny; if you don't want to splash out, go in at around 4pm, when you can simply order a coffee, select a slice of cake from the ample cake buffet, and eat in the fresh air, watching the late afternoon light wink off the cable cars and the grey slopes of the mountain.

Along scenic Kesselberg Road, trade route of the Renaissance, to a one-time centre of transalpine commerce, the beautiful village of Mittenwald.

In 1492, the monks of the **Benediktbeuren** monastery were assigned responsibility for maintaining a considerable stretch of a road that was, in every sense of the word, trail-blazing. The Tyrol, today in Austria and northern Italy, was an important centre of trade in the Middle Ages and Renaissance, a halfway point between the merchants of mighty Venice and their eager customers to the north. Access to the Tyrol from Munich, however, was difficult; the narrow 'King's Path' between the lakes Walchensee and Kochelsee, dating from 1120, was inadequate, and the only other choices were the narrow Isar Valley or the road through the Murnau Swamp, which was all too prone to flooding.

The problem of transportation became acute in 1487, when the hot-tempered Duke of Tyrol arrested 130 Venetian merchants and declared war on the Republic of Venice. The Venetians promptly took their business elsewhere: to the Bavarian town of Mittenwald, which became a flourishing trade centre. For residents of Munich, access to the region was now of even greater importance.

So, at least, thought Heinrich Barth, who had been prospecting for ore, unsuccessfully, in the area of Kochelsee. Barth oversaw the construction of a road, called **Kesselbergstrasse**, hailed even today as an engineering marvel. Now paved, it still makes its winding way across the heights; a roadside plaque pays tribute to Barth's skill and the financial backing of Bavarian Duke Albrecht IV (who, coincidentally, was the one who urged the Tyrolean duke to declare war on Venice in the first place).

Driving south from Munich on the B11, south of Benediktbeuren you'll find the beginning of what's known as Kesselbergstrasse by the flat expanse of **Kochelsee**, where there's a museum devoted to painter **Franz Marc** (open 1 April to 31 October and over Christmas) in the town of **Kochel am See**. After Kochel, a series of zigzags leads you up one mountainside – a lay-by to the right affords a panoramic view of the flat plain stretching away behind you – and down another to a lake of a different colour, **Walchensee**, surrounded by mountains and crowded, during fine weather, with windsurfers. Walchensee is 158m (518ft) higher than Kochelsee, a fact which inspired engineer Oskar von Miller, the founder of

Fair winds on Walchensee

Munich's Deutsches Museum, to undertake the building of a hydroelectric station by Kochelsee. Water from the higher lake is piped over to the lower lake, and has driven the generators of the plant (immediately to the right as you begin the ascent from Kochelsee) since 1924. Kesselbergstrasse's hairpin bends are popular with motorcyclists, who used to flock to the road in such daredevil numbers that they've been barred from southbound passage on weekends.

From Walchensee, you may well be tempted to take the cable car to the top of the **Herzogstand** for a magnificent view of the Alps. Otherwise, continue straight along the B11 to the town of **Mittenwald**, cuddled up against the grey flank of the Karwendel mountain range. As a drive through the surrounding countryside demonstrates (left on the B2 towards Klais, and from there follow signs to **Elmau** to come to a valley whose scenery merits a bit of a detour), Mittenwald has one of the most stunning locations of any village in the Alps. The town itself is fully lovely enough to do justice to its surroundings. Rows of brightly painted houses attest to the fact that Mittenwald has historically been yet another centre for *Lüftlmalers*; a particularly talented local son, Franz Karner, is responsible for facades such as that of the **Neunerhaus** on **Obermarkt**. At one end of this street, where Bavarian restaurants and artisans' shops predominate, a grassy plot of wildflowers supports gnarled apple trees, laden with blossom or green fruit in the spring and summer; at the other end, where Obermarkt meets Hochstrasse, is the **Church of SS Peter and Paul**, a lovely little 18th-century Rococo building with a beautifully frescoed tower.

Before the church there's a monument to the violin maker **Matthias Klotz**. A devoted musician, Klotz went south to Italy to study violin-making in Cremona with the master Amati (Stradivarius's teacher), then wandered about Europe for a few decades before finally returning home to Mittenwald, bringing the tools of his trade with him. His efforts made the town even more renowned than Füssen as the capital of German stringed instrument making, a craft alive and well today (the town's school of violin-making continues to train apprentices from all over the world).

If you would like a more detailed account of the history and practice of this art, be sure to visit the **Geigenbaumuseum** (Museum of Violin-Making) down narrow and picturesque Ballenhausgasse behind the church (Monday to Friday 10am–noon, 2pm–5pm; Saturday–Sunday and holidays 10am–noon; closed November 1 to December 20).

Two forms of sustenance

Seemingly inspired by the curves of the violin, the tower of the Gothic church of **St Nicholas**, on Unter- markt, is another Mitten- wald landmark. Every five years, the town com- memorates its long his- tory of trade with Italy at the two-week Bozener Markt (the next one is 1999) at which vendors, artisans and artists dressed in medieval costume line the Obermarkt offering everything from homemade candles through cast-iron pans to hot mead and bowls of stew.

Straight down Obermarkt, a well-signposted route leads to the **Leutasch Gorge**, where a wooden walkway leads to a remarkable wa- terfall – technically in Austria, but one doesn't split hairs in this bor- der town. Even more breathtaking is another view to which Austria can lay claim – that from the top of the **Karwendel Spitze**, acces- sible by a cable car leaving from the station (about 10 minutes' walk from Obermarkt, behind the railway station) every half hour (November to May 9am–4pm, May to October 8.30am–4.30 or 5pm, depending on the weather). The ride's not long, and the view's spectacular; you can snack at the café atop the mountain. Or save your appetite for dinner at the **Alpenrose** (Obermarkt 1, tel: 08823- 92700), one of Mittenwald's oldest, and most atmospheric, restaurants.

Mittenwald's magnificent setting

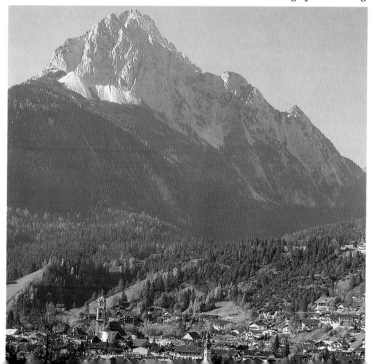

5. Chiemsee

On a ferry round the islands of the largest lake in Bavaria where you can see an 8th-century convent, a gorgeous little fishing village, and yet another of King Ludwig's fantastic castles.

The A8, otherwise known as the Salzburg Autobahn, has got to be one of the most beautiful motorways in the world. Not overly wide, it winds through rolling countryside, past onion-domed churches and red-roofed villages toward a backdrop of the Alps at their most spectacular.

About an hour and a half from Munich, the route runs along the shores of a flat silver plain of water, wrinkled by sailboats and windsurfers, with now and then a hot-air balloon hovering overhead. This is the lake of **Chiemsee**, at 80 sq km (31 sq miles) Bavaria's largest, drawing holidaymakers from all over Germany for sailing, swimming, and other summer pursuits.

To get to the lake, turn off at the Bernau exit (also marked Prien), and follow signs right to **Prien**. Hidden behind the trees, Chiemsee already sheds a silver, liquid light; car parks, campgrounds and hotels called

A church along the A8

'Am See' are indication of its proximity. After about 5km (3 miles), the railway lines and the road lead off left to the town centre (*Ortsmitte*); to the right, a large sign announces ferries to the is-

Morning on Chiemsee

lands and parking for the restaurants and hotels that constitute the settlement of **Stock**. Past a station for the toy-like green steam train that's run since 1887 between the lake and the town of Prien 2km (1 mile) away are the landings for the passenger boats – some of them complete with paddle wheels – out to the islands of Herrenchiemsee and Frauenchiemsee.

Whatever you may think of 'mad' King Ludwig II, no one can say he didn't have an eye for a beautiful setting. In fact, though, he found **Herrenchiemsee**, the island he bought in 1873, unattractive, and hoped to improve its appearance by building a perfect replica of Louis XIV's Versailles. Ludwig, alas, didn't have the funds available to the Sun King (although Louis had modestly limited himself to *one* palace), and only the central wing of the building could be completed before his death in 1886.

Disembarking from the ferry, you will pass a beer garden overlooking the water and the 'old castle', the buildings which housed the Augustinian monastery which originally occupied the island. After a 15-minute walk through woodland and pasture you will see the **castle's** yellow facade through the trees. Complete with marble reception foyer and a magnificent *Spiegelsaal* (Hall of Mirrors), the castle can be visited on half-hour tours through the day (October to March 10am–4pm, April to September 9am–5pm). If you've already seen enough of Ludwig's castles, you may want to content yourself with strolling through the gardens, exploring the island, or visiting the 'old palace', which hosts temporary exhibits in its baroque library. It was here that political leaders met to thrash out the details of the German constitution in 1948.

The 'Spiegelsaal'

From Herrenchiemsee, the ferry route leads past uninhabited Krautinsel, which used to function as a common garden area for the monks and nuns, to **Frauenchiemsee**, where Duke Tassilo III founded a **convent** for Benedictine nuns in 782. The first thing you see as you get off the boat is a sea of flowers; the flowers and herbs used to distill the liqueurs you can buy in the convent shop are all still grown in the convent garden. Today the convent is in use as a boarding school for women studying home economics and child-rearing, and is not open to visitors; but its little church is. Facing the grave-yard, its entrance is framed by wonderful Romanesque carvings, including an image of Tassilo; inside it shows a more recent face due to Gothic and baroque renovations. Nearby is the **Torhalle**, with remnants of 11th-century frescoes, where exhibitions are held.

The island isn't just a convent; it's also home to a small fishing community, and, in recent years, to artists eager for a piece of Fraueninsel's tranquil beauty. At the other end of the island (which is only 600m/1,950ft long and 300m/980ft wide), wander the narrow lanes between the lush banks of flowers which overflow the gardens of every house along the way. Some of these flower-be-decked homes house purveyors of smoked fish (*Räucherfisch*), guest rooms (*Gästezimmer*), or even the island's traditional ceramicist (*Töpferei*), his store windows filled with his work. Take some time to walk around the island, stopping for a meal in the **Gasthof Inselwirt** (Tel: 08054-630) on the water or taking a dip from one of the small beaches before getting on the boat again to continue, ei-ther on the 'Grosse Tour' around the whole lake, or back to Stock.

If you're driving late on the A8 in either direction, watch for the motorway rest stop at the Holzkirchen exit. Unlike the stereo-typical highway eatery, which offers much the same sort of uninspired cafeteria-style food and ambience whether in Germany, England or the States, the **Bayrisches Rasthaus Holzkirchen** (Tel: 08024-93666) is a comfortable restaurant serving a wide range of excellent Bavar-ian food in an appropriately Bavarian atmosphere – a welcome sight to weary drivers returning late to Munich.

Sunset over the lake

6. Berchtesgaden

A tour of the salt mines; Berchtesgaden's Romanesque monastery; and a cruise on tranquil Königssee, the Alps' most beautiful lake.

To non-Germans, unfortunately, the name **Berchtesgaden** is linked with Hitler, who used his nearby home as a weekend retreat during the Third Reich. Actually, the town has closer associations with a certain Mr Perther. About a thousand years ago, Perther built a house (called, in Old German, *Gaden*) here; over the years, Perther's Gaden has been metamorphosed to Berchtesgaden.

The Watzmann towers over Berchtesgaden

Certainly, most of what's interesting about Berchtesgaden pre-dates World War II. Amidst some of the most spectacular scenery in the undeniably scenic Alpine region, the town's sloping streets sport not only the colourful facades common to many Alpine villages, but a number of stunning churches, an 11th-century monastery, and a baroque castle – all above average, even in a region as richly blessed with historical and architectural testimony as Bavaria.

To get to Berchtesgaden, leave the A8 at the Bad Reichenhall exit, and follow the B20. Once in town, you can park, if all else fails, in the underground car park at the city centre. You'll come out just by the **Kurpark**, a lush formal garden which reminds one that this is yet another of the Alps' many *Luftkurort* health resorts; a stroll in the garden is part of the cure. Indeed, the garden exudes a kind of heavy coolness; and its lushness contrasts oddly with the pastel facades which climb the steep cobbled streets.

Make sure you don't miss the opportunity of a visit to the **salt mines**, in operation since 1517. To get there from the garden, cross Schießstättstrasse and follow Bräuhausstrasse

Downtown Berchtesgaden

out of town for about half a mile. In its heyday, this entire region had salt to thank for its economic prosperity; Bad Reichenhall, nearby, still gives its name to German table salt, while it's not hard to see where nearby Salzburg, in Austria, got its name ('salt fortress'). Today, the underground passage is safer than it used to be, and the mines are open to everyone (1½ hour tours 1 May to mid-October daily 9am–5pm; mid-October to 30 April Monday to Saturday 12.30pm–3.30pm, tel: 08652-60020). Donning traditional mining garments, you'll descend into the depths; there, further descent is possible by means of slides (especially popular with children), and a boat will conduct you across a subterranean lake.

After you've seen the salt mines walk back to the town centre and the pedestrian zone on and around **Marktplatz**, a network of cobblestoned streets with everything from handicrafts to grocer's shops. At one end of Marktplatz, a heavy, low arch admits both car and pedestrian traffic to the sudden quiet of **Schlossplatz** (Castle Square). Just before you is the elaborate portal of the **Abbey Church of SS Peter and John the Baptist**, built in 1122 of gold-grey stone; adjacent to this, around two sides of the irregularly-shaped 'square', is the pink facade of the castle itself, brocaded with elaborate white stucco work around the windows. Standing by the fountain and looking back in the direction you came, you can see, in striking contrast to this delicate baroque trim, the heavy arches of an arcade running along one side of the square, which was built as a granary in 1558.

The pastiche effect is continued in the interior of the Abbey Church, which has elements dating from every age between 1122 and 1866, when the towers were finally completed. Soaring columns support a vault suspended over an angular Gothic interior; along the right-hand wall, however, are baroque touches which clearly date from the 17th-century renovation of the castle for the *Fürstpropste* (Prince-priors).

Next door, the **castle** is a real treat. Monastery, royal residence, museum: each of these chapters in the building's history is reflected in some part of the existing architecture. In the cloister, fragile double columns support capitals with fanciful, whimsical carvings of men and animals, indication of the building's Romanesque origins and the Irish roots of Christianity in the region. From here, a flight of stairs leads up to the impressive arched hallway of the **Castle Museum**. Filled with art and armour, frescoes and furniture from medieval to baroque, the castle (guided tours 10am–1pm and 2–5pm;

Alpine attire

St Bartholomä stoops before the Watzmann

closed Saturday Easter to 30 September, at weekends and holidays October to Easter) actually remained a Wittelsbach residence until the death of Crown Prince Rupprecht in 1955.

Head back to your car and follow the B20, which forks off to the left from the train station toward Schönau and Königssee. Walkers can cover the 3km (2 miles) to Königsee on foot, along a path which starts near the railway station and leads along the stream. Rising steeply to the left of the road is the peak of Hitler's 'Eagle's Nest' retreat, the **Kehlsteinhaus**.

Königssee, the King's Lake, is quite simply one of the most beautiful spots in the Alps. Flat, silent, mirror-still, the narrow lake is surrounded by mountains. You can see the lake from look-out points on shore, such as **Malerwinkel** (painter's corner), or one of the electric passenger boats which operate year-round (except when the lake is iced over). Although the **Watzmann** mountains (mother, father, and seven children) dominate the panorama from almost any vantage point, it is from the boat that you'll get one of the most stunning views. Halfway down the lake is the little chapel of **St Bartholomä**, its round domes outlined against one of the most beautiful backdrops you could hope to find. The summit of the Watzmann towers 2,100m (6,800ft) above, its giant east face the highest in the Eastern Alps. Rain or shine, there's something ethereal about this beautiful cruise. (Summer every 20 minutes 8am–5.30pm; pre- and post-season every 15–30 minutes after 8.15am; winter every 45 minutes 9.45am–3.30pm).

Leaving Königssee, either retrace your steps or cut through the village of Schönau to get to the B305, the **German Alpine Road** (*Deutsche Alpenstrasse*). This scenic route winds through green valleys and wooded slopes along the Alps; you're heading towards the valley village of **Ramsau**, with its much-photographed jewel of a baroque church. Stay on the 305, however, and turn off to the right (following signs to Hochschwarzeck) up a zig-zagging road to the **Hotel-Gasthof Nutzkaser** (Tel: 08657-388), where you can enjoy a wonderful Bavarian meal 1,100m (3,600ft) above sea level, with a panoramic view of the mountains.

The Romantic Road

When the sleepy, forgotten walled towns of medieval, half-timbered houses which dot Western Bavaria were rediscovered by 19th-century travellers, they rapidly became popular tourist spots where people could capture the flavour of days gone by. Today, the route leading from Ludwig's castles in the south to Würzburg in the north has been christened the 'Romantic Road'. From the road you can glimpse castle towers and church spires before driving into the towns themselves, still fundamentally unchanged, although the crush of tourism has made them appear a little less sleepy than they did a century ago.

Reflections of Dinkelsbühl

We have already covered the southern section of the route in itinerary 2; in the three day itineraries that follow, you can see more of its most important highlights. We begin in Augsburg, once a powerful free city of the Holy Roman Empire, and continue northwards along the B25 through medieval Dinkelsbühl and Rothenburg and on to Würzburg, residence of a long line of prince-bishops and the home of Franconian wine.

7. Augsburg

A tour of the city from Renaissance town hall to Gothic cathedral; Europe's earliest council flats; the shops of medieval craftsmen; and the homes of Brecht, Holbein, and the family Mozart.

Founded in 15BC, Augsburg has gone through many ups and downs since Tacitus described it as the 'most splendid colony of the province of Rhaetium'. An independent city-state of the Holy Roman Empire since 1156, the city flourished in the Renaissance with such artisan trades as gold- and silversmithing; but its power gradually waned until Napoleon bequeathed it to Bavaria in 1806. In this century, World War II bombings virtually razed it to the ground. But rebuilders and restorers have been hard at work, and Augsburg today has both the narrow canals and ivy-draped city walls of the old city and, on the other hand, the businesses and commerce of a modern urban centre.

Augsburg's Town Hall

Start your tour of Augsburg at the square before the **Rathaus** (Town Hall); completed in 1620, it's one of Germany's major Renaissance constructions. Its architect, Elias Holl, also designed the neighbouring **Perlach Tower**, which you can climb (Christmas, Easter and 1 May to 31 October) for a view of the city and its surroundings. In his 20 years as the city's master builder, Holl planned a number of major Augsburg buildings; but in 1631, he was ignominiously removed from office because he was Protestant – despite Augsburg's historic position of religious tolerance.

At the centre of the square water splashes from one of three **fountains** commissioned for Augsburg's 1600th birthday – in 1589. The three statues depict Augustus, symbol of the city founders; Mercury (commerce and trade); and Hercules (Man's mastery of Nature): it's Augustus you see here.

Follow Karolinenstrasse north toward the city's magnificent **Cathedral** (*Dom*), begun in the 9th century, and redone in Gothic style in the 14th. The cast bronze plates on the door to the left of the main entrance, depicting Old Testament and various mythological scenes, are thought to date from around 1050. Inside, the stained-glass windows of the prophets in Jewish costume, supposedly installed when the church was renovated in 1140, are said to be the oldest in the world. You can also see some altar paintings by local son Hans Holbein the Elder.

North along Frauentorstrasse is the **Mozart House**, today a museum, where Leopold Mozart, father of the composer Wolfgang Amadeus, was born and raised. Continue on to the street Pfärrle and turn right to come to the **Church of St Gall**, the oldest in Augsburg, built in 1051 and re-

A resident of the Fuggerei

stored in the 15th century, sitting against the old **city walls**. It's more a matter of legend than fact that Martin Luther escaped through the hole in the wall behind the church when he fled Augsburg in 1518; but the hole is there, plain to see.

Further south, past the 1504 house of painter Hans Burgkmair on your right, cross Leonhardsberg, and turn down Auf dem Rain, a narrow street of low terrace houses traversed by a miniature canal. In **house No 7**, playwright Bertolt Brecht was born in 1898. Today, there are art exhibits on the ground floor and a collection of Brecht memorabilia above (May to September 10am–5pm, October to April 10am–4pm, closed Monday).

Across the street (house number 6) and up the street (Schmiedgasse 15) are the Goldsmith's Shop and the Bookbinder's. These are two of the stops along Augsburg's **Artisan Route** (*Handwerkerweg*), a tour through workshops and stores where certain trades have been plied for centuries, including the violin-makers, the tannery, and the convent where nuns embroider clerical garments for festive High Masses. Not all of the stops along the route are open every day, but some observe normal business hours. For details, pick up the pamphlet *Ausburger Handwerkerweg* at the tourist office.

Barfüsserstrasse, to the left, leads to the entrance to the **Fuggerei**. Jakob Fugger (1459–1525), the scion of a prosperous family of businessmen, brought their already thriving empire to new heights. But Fugger was not just a money-bagging tycoon; as proof of this, he built the first council flats in Europe. Founded in 1516, this development for poor Catholics charged an annual rent of one florin for each three-room apartment, one condition being that residents say the Lord's Prayer every day for the souls of the Fuggers. Both the rent (DM1.72) and this condition have survived to the present day. For a local meal in a rustic atmosphere, try the **Fuggerei-Stube** (Jakoberstrasse 26, Tel: 0821-30870) for lunch.

Retrace your steps along Jakoberstrasse and Barfüsserstrasse before turning left down Mittlerer Lech

Afra's Cathedral

for a stroll along the Lech canals (which have run through the city since the days of the Romans), past old buildings like the 18th-century **Gignoux House**. To your left is the Gothic **Vogel Gate** in the city walls. Continue down Schwibbogengasse, past the water wheel; a short cut left off Margaretenstrasse leads to the **Heilig-Geist-Spital**, designed by the ubiquitous Holl, today home to the **Augsburg Puppet Theatre** and the **Swabian Crafts Museum** (highlight of the Artisan Route). A short walk brings you to the **Rotes Tor** (Red Gate), built in the 16th century as a defensive fortification to safeguard the vital trade route to Italy, and renovated according to Holl's designs in 1622. In the Middle Ages, a vital source of city water were the **Water Towers** on the left, which date back to the 1400s.

Up Ulrichsgasse, you'll come to the **Cathedral of St Ulrich and St Afra**. Afra ran a brothel in Augusta Vindelicorum in the 3rd century; one night, a Spanish bishop fleeing persecution in his own country took refuge in her establishment and converted her and her daughters to Christianity, and she became so zealous that she and her offspring were burnt at the stake in 304.

Fountain detail

Her remains are ensconced, together with those of Ulrich, in the crypt of her soaring cathedral. Ulrich, the first man to be canonised in the history of the Catholic church, gave his name to both this Catholic church and the adjacent, but much smaller, Protestant **Ulrich's Church**. The two churches are a nod to Augsburg's 1555 law of religious tolerance, which decreed that the ruler of the land had to choose one religion, and his subjects were obliged to follow him – a measure which predictably gave rise to no end of trouble.

From Ulrichsplatz, broad Maximilianstrasse runs back toward the Town Hall. Across from the **Hercules Fountain** on the left is the **Schaezler Palais**, built by an 18th-century businessman. The yellow-fronted building houses a rococo festival hall, a marvellous staircase, and two museums, of which I find the **State Gallery**, featuring a portrait of Fugger by Albrecht Dürer, the more compelling.

At the Mercury Fountain, cut across the pedestrian zone to Martin-Luther-Platz and the **Church of St Anne**, a monastery which turned Protestant during the Reformation, and gave shelter to Martin Luther during his ill-starred visit to Augsburg in 1518; it now contains the well-known portrait of Luther by Lucas Cranach the Elder. Back on Karolinenstrasse, the **König von Flandern Brauerei** (downstairs at No 12, tel: 0821-158050) serves snacks and its own home-brewed beer.

A glance at the flower-draped town of Dinkelsbühl and its Gothic church; then a plunge into history in medieval Rothenburg with its Renaissance town hall and Cathedral; a museum of crime; and half-timbered houses galore. You'll need a car.

Romantic Road
40 km / 25 miles

It's hard to find anything much more romantic than the stretch of the Romantic Road between Nördlingen, Dinkelsbühl and Rothenburg ob der Tauber. North of Augsburg, the B25 affords glimpses of castle towers and church spires before leading you through 16th-century walled towns, their half-timbered facades laden with geraniums.

But the drive is nothing compared to a walk around the towns themselves. A traveller with time to spare will want to tarry in each of the three mentioned above; if you have only a day, look at Dinkelsbühl in the morning, then go on to lovely Rothenburg. Be warned that this town, the undisputed pearl of the Romantic Road, is also its undisputed tourist attraction, extremely crowded on weekends and holidays.

Dinkelsbühl's picturesque main square is a feast for the eye. In summer, the house facades are buried in flowers; in winter, the snow-clad gables have the smug serenity of a Christmas card. Across from the red building of the tourist office, **St George's Cathedral** is a Gothic masterpiece with delicate clusters of pillars and jewel-like stained-glass win-

Flowery facade in Dinkelsbühl

dows. On the other side of Marktplatz notice the **Deutsches Haus** (German House), built by the Drexler family in order to demonstrate their new status when they were elevated to the nobility in 1556. The six-storey, half-timbered house with its asymmetric facade today houses a restaurant.

Behind St George's, a narrow street leads to the **Wörnitz Gate** in the old city walls. These 14th-century fortifications were only preserved thanks to King Ludwig I, who intervened when the citizens began pulling them down to use the stone as building material in the 19th century. In front of the gateway, the lion on the medieval **Lion Fountain** displays his tongue in a threatening roar. Go through the gate and cross the footbridge for a look at the walls from the outside, mirrored in the calm water.

From here, a footpath follows the walls around to the left, where you can re-enter the city by way of the little street Badgässlein, coming out by the old Spital (home for the sick and elderly). Built in 1280, this rambling collection of buildings around a green, park-like yard still houses a home for old people, as well as the city's **Historical Museum**, its collection devoted to local lore and lifestyles through the ages, a concert hall and a public sauna: all in all, a remarkably successful integration of the historical into modern daily life.

Medieval Rothenburg

The Spital fronts on Dr-Martin-Luther-Strasse, which leads back to the centre of town. Up Steingasse to your right is the restaurant/hotel **Weisses Ross** (Steingasse 12, Tel: 09851-2274), which serves a very good lunch. This establishment's new annexe is located in an inventively converted stable; clean modern and luxurious rooms still display the heavy beams and dormer windows of the former farming facility.

Suitably refreshed and heading north from Dinkelsbühl on the B25, you'll pass the turn-off to another lovely romantic town, Feuchtwangen, on the hour-long drive to **Rothenburg ob der Tauber**. Perched high above ('ob') the Tauber river, this enchanting town looks as if its 1274 city charter had been issued

All roads lead to the Market Square

only yesterday; the sole indications of modernity are the tour buses parked outside the walls. Leave your car with the buses near **Galgentor** (Gallows Gate), part of the second, 14th-century ring of city defences. As you walk toward the city centre you will pass through part of the earlier, 12th-century fortifications: the **Weisse Turm** (White Tower), near which a small garden lined with Jewish gravestones is dedicated to Rabbi Meir ben Baruch, a 13th-century Talmudic scholar.

All roads in Rothenburg lead to **Marktplatz** (Market Square). To your right, the 1446 tavern (built for the city councillors) features, on the outside, a double-faced clock from 1683 as well as a set of mechanical figures who enact the most famous incident of Rothenburg's history several times a day (hourly 11am–3pm and 8–10pm). During the Thirty Years' War, in 1631, General Tilly and his Catholic League troops were retreating through Protestant Rothenburg. Fearing certain destruction, the Mayor of Rothenburg, Nusch, made a bet with Tilly: if he could down the contents of a goblet filled with 3¼ litres of wine at one gulp, Tilly would spare his town. Tilly agreed, the mayor emptied the goblet and the rest is history.

Dominating the square is the Town Hall, its 1570s Renaissance facade built when a wing of the older, Gothic section of the building burnt down in 1501. The building's other original wing, built in the 13th and 14th centuries, fronts Herrengasse, on your left. With a height of 60m (200ft), the old tower offers a great

Riemenschneider's Altar of the Holy Blood

The hotel is behind the church

view to anyone in excellent physical shape, but its narrow stairs are not for the faint-hearted.

Walk behind the square to the right to find the **St-Jakobs-Kirche** (Church of St James). This 14th-century church gets so much light from its tall windows that even the brilliant stained-glass around the altar seems dark by comparison. Against the flat, white stone, the carved wood of the altarpieces and chancel comes especially alive. Not that the craftsmanship of Tilman Riemenschneider needs such a contrast to appear lifelike. Up the steps at the back of the nave is the chapel housing his **Altar of the Holy Blood**, whose carved figures are so strongly individual that they seem to breathe, while the angels appear poised for immediate flight on their soaring wings. Atop the altar, a gold reliquary from 1270 contains a drop of the precious fluid for which it's named.

While almost equal in height, the church's two towers are quite different in appearance; legend has it that the southern tower was built by the master builder, and the northern one by his apprentice. Furious that his student's work was better than his own, the master flung himself from the southern tower to his death.

If you're ready for a break at this stage, the tree-shaded garden of the **Hotel Reichs-Küchenmeister** (Kirchplatz 8–10, tel: 09861-9700) to your right, overlooking the back of the church, is a pleasant, if well-frequented, place to stop.

If you want to keep going a bit longer, then Klingengasse leads right under the Holy Blood Chapel to **St Wolfgang**, one of the more unusual churches you'll encounter in Bavaria. This shepherds' church is built into the city walls; twisting staircases give access to the walls above (where, once you have passed through the low-ceilinged Shepherds' Dance Museum, you can see the 'Pitch-Face' (Pechnase) stone face through whose mouth hot pitch used to be poured down on would-be attackers) and the defensive underground passageways below. To the right of the main altar is the **Wendelin Altar**, which is dedicated to the shepherds' patron saint. Notice the shallow groove in the stone at the front where defenders of the town, called to arms, sharpened their swords while blessing them at the same time.

Leaving the church, bear right and walk outside the walls, looking down across the Tauber river at the funny little tower built as a weekend getaway by Rothenburg's most popular Mayor, Heinrich Toppler, in 1388. Ahead of you, on the narrow spur at the western extremity of the Old Town is the **Burggarten** (Castle Garden), occupying the site of the town's 10th-century castle, which was destroyed by an earthquake in 1356. From the green, shaded lawns you can look down and see the double-arched bridge over the Tauber, built in the 14th century. Inside the **Burgtor** (Castle Gate), the first turning

Creatively carved timb

left leads to the **Burg Hotel** (Klostergasse 1–3, tel: 09861-5037), whose gorgeous, individually-furnished rooms all command a piece of the view.

Running along the southern wall, Burggasse leads to the former monastery which houses Rothenburg's unique **Museum of Crime** (April to October 9.30am–6pm; November, January, February 2pm–4pm; December and March 10am–4pm). Devoted to instruments of torture and punishment through the ages, the museum is filled with exhibits carefully explained in both German and English, offering a diverting look at another side of daily life in the Middle Ages.

The Burgtor leads into the castle

Bustling Schmiedgasse leads, to the right, to Rothenburg's most popular and most photographed landmark, the **Plönlein**. This consists of a fork in the road leading to two of the city's hallmark gateways, separated by a half-timbered house. If you want to get away from the crowd, continue along the walls until you come to the **Spital**; here, you will be left alone to investigate the lovely old buildings and the Gothic carvings of the tiny **Church of the Holy Ghost** in peace.

A fine dinner in the **Hotel Goldener Hirsch** (Untere Schmiedgasse 16–25, tel: 09861-7080) will fortify your body and soul after a long day of sightseeing.

9. Würzburg

A residence fit for a bishop; a bridge across the Main and the House of Franconian Wine; a mighty fortress; and dinner in a medieval flower garden.

Although it's been home to Bishops since the bishopric was established in 742, the Franconian city of **Würzburg** didn't have its true flowering until after the 16th century. Prince-Bishop Julius Echter of Mespelbrunn (1573–1617) founded the first University and the Juliusspital for the poor (but also encouraged witch-hunts and persecution of the Jews); the 17th and 18th centuries were dominated by the Schönborn family, patrons of the arts who oversaw the building of the Residence.

The stairwell of the Residenz

Liquid refreshment, as well as art, has its own flavour in this northernmost corner of Bavaria. As the south is famous for beer, Lower Franconia is famous for its wine, which comes in distinctive round bottles called *Bocksbeutel* (a vernacular term for the reproductive organs of goats).

The best place to start in Würzburg and the showpiece of the city is the Prince-Bishop's palatial **Residenz**. For years, the Prince-Bishops had lived in the fortress of Marienburg; but Johann Philipp

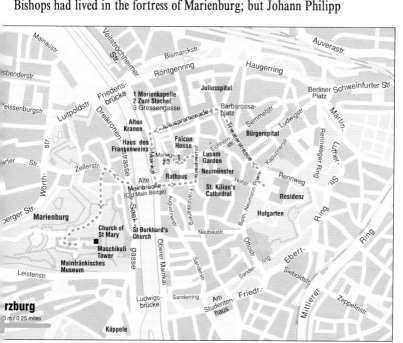

Franz von Schönborn, who took office in 1714, wanted to be more in the centre of things, and commissioned 33-year-old Balthasar Neumann to build him a suitable abode. A host of builders and artists were drawn into the 25-year project, one of them responsible for the world's largest fresco above the magnificent double staircase, Giovanni Battista Tiepolo.

After visiting the interior (guided tours of the furnished rooms, including the Hofkirche, a Neumann jewel with Tiepolo trimming, April to October 9am–5pm, November to March 10am–4pm), walk through the Residence's wonderful formal gardens. If you're in the city in June, you may catch one of the torchlit outdoor performances of the annual **Mozart Festival**.

Walking up Theaterstrasse from the Residence, you'll come to the **Bürgerspital**, founded in 1319 and still in use both as a home for the poor and elderly and a wine-cellar where you can eat and drink well and inexpensively (Bürgerspital Weinstuben, Theaterstrasse 19, tel: 0931-352880). Residents of the Bürgerspital still receive one free glass of wine every day as a part of their keep.

Turn left at Barbarossaplatz into the Juliuspromenade which runs

Cross the river to the Marienburg

by the **Juliusspital**, a palace built by Petrini after Julius's original 1576 building burnt down in 1699. A rococo apothecary's is preserved on the ground floor; while, true to Spital tradition, there's a wine-cellar in the basement (Juliusspital Weinstuben, Juliuspromenade 19, tel: 0931-54080). Straight ahead, you can see the **Alten Kranen**, the old crane on the river Main dating from 1773; next to it, at the **Haus des Frankenweins** (House of Franconian Wine, Kranenkai 1, tel: 0931-390110), you can sample a variety of local vintages.

Proceed along the Mainkai to the picturesque **Alte Mainbrücke** (Old Main Bridge), with its statue of St Kilian. Cross the river here to come to the beginning of the steep path up to the fortress of **Marienburg**. Although the city has known defeat, the fortress, locals say, has never been taken by military force; treachery opened the gates to conquering Swedish troops in the Thirty Years' War. On the grassy slopes around the walls there's a monument to the Peasants' Revolt of 1525, in which the lower classes attempted to storm the fortress by burying explosives under its walls, an undertaking as bloody as it was futile.

Once you've climbed the path, commence your tour of the fortress with the **Mainfränkisches Museum** (open daily April to October

10am–5pm, November to March 10am–4pm), whose exhibits include an amazing collection of statuary by local son Tilman Riemenschneider. Riemenschneider (1460–1531) was a highly regarded artist during his active career, so popular that he was elected Würzburg's Mayor in 1520; siding, however, with the peasants in the 1525 uprising, he was imprisoned and tortured, and never worked again. Politics and art don't mix.

Architectural testimonials from every era are present in the buildings comprising the fortress. Earliest of all is the **Church of St Mary** with its round chapel, dating from 704, at the centre of the main courtyard; the latest (excepting post-war reconstruction) is also round, Balthasar Neumann's 1728 **Maschikuli Tower** on the south side of the walls, facing Neumann's hillside chapel **Käppele** further upstream, a famous pilgrimage church devoted to the Holy Virgin. You can also see the Renaissance well-house, and the tower where Riemenschneider was held prisoner.

Once you've finished in the fortress, descend to the Saalgasse, which runs alongside the river Main past the home of the Fishermen's Guild (founded in 1010) on the left to St **Burkhard's Church**. The interior of this church includes 19th-century frescoes by the altar, Gothic choir stalls with marvellous angels' heads on the back, a Riemenschneider Madonna, and a long, chunky Romanesque nave with round arches.

Retrace your steps to recross the Old Main Bridge and pass the city's 12th-century **Rathaus** (Town Hall) and Sternplatz, once the heart of the tradesmens' district (as the names of surrounding streets like Doctor Street or Cobbler Street indicate), towards the Cathedral. **St Kilian's Cathedral** was another casualty of war; the reconstructed version gives an idea of its prototype and displays many of its original art treasures. Among these, of course, are works by both Riemenschneider and Balthasar Neumann; Riemenschneider's

memorial stone is also located in the Cathedral (or a copy of it; the original is in the museum), on the north wall. Examination reveals just how scarce funds were in this once-prosperous family after the master's death: there was no money for a new

The distinctive 'Bocksbeutel'

The Falcon House

stone for his son, and his father's had to do double duty with the addition of the younger man's name along the bottom when he died.

Up Kürschnerhof you can see the facade of the **Neumünster** on the right, which was 'baroque-ised' in 1720. Although the Würzburg Cathedral is dedicated to St Kilian, it's this church which was built over the saint's grave. There is another significant grave behind the church in peaceful **Lusam Garden**: that of the medieval poet and troubadour Walther von der Vogelweide. His surname means 'bird-meadow', and the lid of his tomb contains four hollows which collect water for the birds.

The next turn on the left brings you to the yellow **Falcon House**, its stuccoed baroque facade exactly reconstructed after the 1751 original. Ahead of you, the tall late Gothic church is the 15th-century **Marienkapelle** (Mary's Chapel). Over its south door are copies of Riemenschneider's *Adam and Eve* (the originals are displayed in the museum), while the north side door features an even more unusual ornament: faced with the challenge of physically depicting the Immaculate Conception, the sculptor showed God impregnating the Virgin by means of a tube running into her ear.

Down Marktgasse and left onto Gressengasse, and you'll arrive at **Zum Stachel** (Gressengasse 1, tel: 0931-52770) in time for dinner. First mentioned in 1413, this famous restaurant was frequented by Riemenschneider and his cronies, and its proprietor hid peasants fleeing after the 1525 uprising. Its outdoor courtyard, an effusion of stone arches and geraniums, seems more like a stage set than a piece of history, but you can't go wrong here dining under the stars. Later on, you can walk past Riemenschneider's former residence at Franziskanergasse 1 (now the restaurant Pfeffermühle) on your way to the night spots that line Sanderstrasse.

A truly Immaculate Conception

Franconia

Seeing the beauties of Würzburg may inspire you to explore more of the three provinces of Franconia (Franken). The name *Franken* actually dates back to 531, when the Frankish ruler Theodoric conquered the Thuringian empire and absorbed it into his own Frankish empire, *Frankenreich*. Comprising the northern section of Bavaria, Upper, Middle and Lower Franconia are regions with their own dialect, their own mores, even their own cuisine. The important and historic cities of Bamberg, Nuremberg and Bayreuth can all be easily reached by public transport. The following itineraries ensure you get a taste of the region's beautiful countryside as well by including a tour through the *Fränkische Schweiz* (Franconia's 'little Switzerland'), for which you'll need a car.

10. Bamberg

A medieval city which smokes its beer, has a town hall in the middle of its river, and boasts Germany's most marvellous cathedral.

Called the 'treasure chest of Franconia', Bamberg is an ideal city to use as a base while you explore this region. Gothic churches, baroque palaces, and half-timbered artisans' houses with 15th-century dates over their doorways all contribute to the city's visual charm, as do the flowering riverside balconies of the neighbourhood nicknamed 'Little Venice'. A seat of art and culture since its founding in 1007, and one of Germany's first printing centres, Bamberg has preserved this heritage with its university, theatre, and the Bamberg Symphony, widely known as one of Germany's finest orchestras. At night, people meet in the city's pubs for another local speciality, smoked beer (*Rauchbier*).

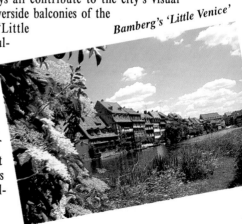

Bamberg's 'Little Venice'

If you've come by car, one of the city's many well-marked car parks is on Schillerplatz, the broad square where the **E.T.A. Hoffmann Theatre** is located. Author, playwright, and would-be composer, Hoffmann (1776–1822) was long a resident of Bamberg, employed by the city theatre; today, he's best known for his stories, familiar to many as *The Tales of Hoffmann*. The house where he lived for four years, **Schillerplatz 26**, is today a museum.

At the end of the square, follow Richard Wagner Strasse to Non-

The Town Hall on the river

nenbruecke, then turn up Am Kanal. Before long, you'll sight the **Town Hall**, perched on an islet in the river Regnitz, its older, half-timbered section appended to a taller, baroque abdomen. Originally dating from 1461, the building was 'baroque-ised' in the 1700s; additions from this period include the tower and murals depicting classical heroes and significant Bambergers ensconced in flourishes of architectural *trompe l'oeil*.

For the best view of the Town Hall, cross the first bridge on your left before the building and stand on the tip of the island just across from it. As you face the Town Hall, **Geyersworth Castle** is right behind you. Now home to city administration offices, the medieval palace with its ivy-covered courtyard and fountain was rebuilt in the 1500s by the Prince-Bishops, who lived there until the construction of the New Residence in 1697.

Return to Nonnenbruecke and cross the river to Concordiastrasse. A right will bring you to an uphill intersection and the yellow baroque facade of the **Böttinger House** (1707–13). As you begin the steep ascent on the street called Eisgrube, notice the doorknob on **house No 14**: a wizened, smiling face, polished by use over the years. This doorknob was immortalised in Hoffmann's story *The Golden Pot*, in which it began to speak to the protagonist as he moved to enter the building.

To the right, a flight of steps ascends to the 14-century Church of Our Lady, more commonly known as **Obere Pfarre** (Upper Parish Church), a Gothic wonder bearing the baroque traces of the 17th century. As the church's special religious festival is the Assumption of the Virgin, it's fitting that it owns a painting of this event by Tintoretto, hanging on the back wall of the right-hand aisle. Even better is the 14th-century

The talking doorknob

Tabernacle, in a chapel behind
the high altar, carved with row
upon row of figures depicting
the Entombment of Christ, the
Apostles, and the Last Judgment.
Outside, a porch on the north side
of the building depicts the Wise
and Foolish Virgins (the wise ones
looking appropriately self-righteous,
the foolish ones with a slightly
bovine air).

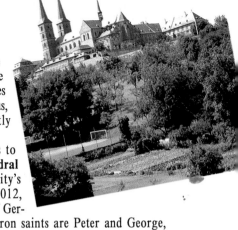

From here you can cut across to
to Bamberg's showpiece **Cathedral**
(*Dom*). Built atop one of the city's
seven hills and consecrated in 1012,
this is one of the masterpieces of Ger-
man sacred architecture. Its patron saints are Peter and George,
but its interior is more markedly influenced by the ubiquitous sculp-
tors Veit Stoss and Tilman Riemenschneider, the former with his dark
wooden **Christmas Altar** in the left transept, and the latter with
his **tomb of Heinrich and Kunigunde** (the city's patron saints and
founders) at the centre of the Cathedral.

Neither of these masters, however, was responsible for the most
famous sculpture in the city: no one knows who created the ethereal **Bamberger Reiter**. Said by some to represent the ideal of Chris-
tian knights in the Middle Ages, this unknown and beautiful horseman
sits his mount in a niche high above the ground, at the rear end
of the building.

Across from the Cathedral is the rambling **New Residence**, commissioned by the Bishop of Bamberg and Elector of Mainz, Lothar
Franz von Schönborn, in 1697. Its splendid tapestries and furnish-
ings can be seen by taking a tour (April to September 9am–noon and
1.30–5pm, October to March until 4pm). One special highlight is
the richly ornamented **Emperor's Room** (*Kaisersaal*), where the
Bamberg Symphony occasionally stages candlelight concerts. Through
the main archway is the **Rose Garden**, in summer a veritable blan-
ket of scented blooms, commanding a panoramic view over the city
from its outdoor café tables (Café Im Rosengarten, open May to
October).

Next to the cathedral is the original imperial and bishop's palace,
the **Old Court** (*Alte Hofhaltung*). The Renaissance **Ratstube** faces
the square; through the gateway, the courtyard is wonderfully picturesque, with all the half-timbers, gables and flowers a photogra-
pher could desire. Formerly the seat of city government, the building
now houses Bamberg's **History Museum**.

From Domplatz a narrow flight of stairs leads down to the old
town; if you descend, you'll come to the quintessential Bamberg
eatery, **Schlenkerla** (Dominikanerstrasse 6, tel: 0951-56060). This
traditional restaurant has been producing its own Rauchbier since

1678; the building itself is a couple of centuries older.

Another hill, another church: but the view alone makes the ascent up to the former Benedictine monastery of **St Michael's** worthwhile (go out the rear of the Alte Hofhaltung to Domstrasse, and keep going up). The abbey was founded in 1012, but today's buildings went up in the 17th and 18th centuries. Unusual features include a ceiling frescoed with the images of over 600 medicinal herbs, and the tomb of St Otto behind the high altar (some say that creeping through its small opening is a sure cure for either backache or lumbago).

In the former brewery, the **Franconian Brewing Museum** (Thursday to Sunday 1–4pm, April to October only) explores the history of the monastic breweries, which were once a thriving industry but crippled by the secularisation of 1803 (today, only a handful of establishments, such as Ettal in itinerary 3, continue the ancient brewing tradition).

One landmark of the region isn't in Bamberg at all. Back in the car, follow Obere Königsstrasse to the B173 toward Lichtenfels. About 30km (18 miles) on is the turnoff to the **Vierzehnheiligen**, the church of Fourteen Saints, considered by some to be Balthasar Neumann's greatest work. Flecked with

Inside the Vierzehnheiligen

gold and blue, the scrolled white interior is built around a mammoth shrine, said to have miracle-working properties, with depictions of all 14 of the eponymous saints. The breathtaking weath of rococo ornamentation and frescoes adorn a structural plan that is an achievement in itself: the building's ground plan is based on a series of interlocking ovals, a touch that is at once supremely baroque and an architectural *tour de force*. Whether you're more taken with the sculptures or the structure, the building is an absolute masterpiece.

If you are planning to stay in this part of Bavaria for the evening, return to Bamberg where you will find a taste of genuine local cuisine at the restaurant **Brudermühle** (Schranne 1, tel: 0951-955220).

From the former Residence city and Wagner temple of Bayreuth, past caves, cliffs and castles to the mountaintop church of Gössweinstein, the towering rocks of Tüchersfeld, and the half-timbered houses of medieval Forchheim.

Lovers of music know **Bayreuth** as the site of the annual Richard Wagner summer opera festival, and the place where the eccentric composer made his home. But the small city had aspirations to cultural grandeur even before Wagner arrived in 1874. In 1731, Wilhelmine, favourite sister of Frederick the Great, married the Margrave of Bayreuth and set out to convert the town she saw as a 'dung heap' into a residence befitting her cosmopolitan tastes.

Coming up from the large car park behind the Stadthalle (which hosts concerts and theatrical events), you're right around the corner from the **Neues Schloss** (New Palace), one of Wilhelmine's last projects, built in 1755 (tours April to September 10–11.20am and 1.30–4.10pm; October to March until 2.50pm, closed Monday). The Margravine Wilhelmine's *tour de force* is located a little further down Ludwigstrasse, which becomes

Richard Wagner

Opernstrasse: the **Markgräfisches Opernhaus** (Margrave's Opera House) is a three-tiered baroque extravaganza (tours April to September 9–11.30am and 1.30–4.30pm, October to March 10–11.30am

The Festspielhaus

and 1.30–3pm, closed Monday). The multi-faceted Margravine was herself a musician who played four instruments and composed an opera; she was also an avid student of philosophy, founding the *Friedrichsakademie* (destined to evolve into the University of Erlangen) in 1742.

Across from the theatre is the **Old Castle**, home to the margraves until 1754, reconstructed after 1945 bombings and today housing city administration offices. Behind the castle, you can rest your feet at an outdoor café before embarking on the 15-minute walk from Luitpoldplatz along Bahnhofstrasse to the **Festspielhaus** (Festival Theatre). Bayreuth's claim to international fame, this house, opened in 1876, is virtually a required sight for visitors to the area. Not that its plain brick exterior would in itself merit this kind of attention. Wagner wanted the focus of his theatre to be the events on stage, rather than the ornamentation – as anyone who's spent four hours sitting on one of the auditorium's bare wooden seats knows all too well. What was saved on decoration was put into the stage machinery, trail-blazing then and still remarkable today; the theatre's acoustics are also among the best in the world. Performances of Wagner's operas are given in August; tickets are almost impossible to get, but you can tour the theatre throughout the year (daily 10–10.45am and 2.15–3pm, closed November).

If you're intrigued by the single-mindedness of a man who expected politicians to provide him with funds to indulge his creative desires, stop in at Wagner's home, **Haus Wahnfried** (1874), on your way back to your car. Located off Richard-Wagner-Strasse, the villa is today a Wagner Museum, filled with memorabilia (including the composer's piano) testifying to Wagner's eccentricities as well as his strengths. Recordings of the Wagner operas are played at 10am, 12pm, and 2pm.

Back in the car, follow the B2 south to the town of **Pegnitz**, renowned among international visitors principally for the luxurious **Pflaums Posthotel Pegnitz** (Nürnberger Strasse 12–16, tel: 09241-7250). Its restaurant Pflaumengarten serves up *haute cuisine* interpretations of regional food; for a less expensive foray into fine Frankish fare, there's the Posthalterstube, also in the hotel.

From Pegnitz, the B470 leads straight through the heart of one

mill in Ebermannstadt

of my favourite Bavarian regions: Franconia's **Little Switzerland** (*Fränkische Schweiz*), so called because of the resemblance which its rocky cliffs, vivid green hills and tumbling rivers bear to the original. In addition to some of Bavaria's most wonderful – and unusual – landscapes, the region is chock-a-block with castles, churches, and caves. In fact, the **Teufelshöhle** (Devil's Cave), on your left after about 9km (5 miles), is the largest cave in Germany – which won't come as a surprise once you see the yawning cave mouth on the other side of the river. This underground limestone labyrinth of glistening stalactites and stalagmites (the former, by the way, are the ones that hang from the ceiling; the latter, those that grow up from the ground) is open Easter through October 9am–5pm, November to 23 December Tuesday and Saturday 10am–noon, for 40-minute tours.

Nearby **Pottenstein** is overshadowed by an enormous cliff topped with dwellings. Just before you reach the village, a road on the right leads up to the **Burg** (Castle), originally dating from 918, and still inhabited today (visible on guided tours during the summer season). To see the village's historic centre, turn right on Forchheimer Strasse and park by the river to stroll along the *Hauptstrasse* (main street) and the market place.

From Pottenstein, the B470 leads to **Tüchersfeld**. You'll see the remarkable cliff formations before you see the little town nestled beneath them: resembling some sort of giant mushroom growth, the rounded pillars of rock, crowned with flags and even a little house, tower spectacularly over the river valley below. Before you come to them, a road leads right to the **Fränkische Schweiz Museum**, devoted to the geology, culture, history, and Jewish heritage of the region (April to October Tuesday to Sunday 10am–5pm, November to March Sunday only 1.30–5pm). Opposite the museum turn-off, on an islet in the river Püttlach, is the half-timbered **Old Mill** (*Mühle*).

At the village of **Beringersmühle**, the three river valleys of the Fränkische Schweiz – the Wiesenttal, the Ailsbachtal, and the Püttlachtal – come together. From here, the car ascent to **Gössweinstein** is short but steep, rewarded by the sight of the yellow exterior of yet another fine building by Balthasar Neumann. Dedicated to (and named after) the shrine of the Holy Trinity which it houses, the **church**, begun in 1739, looks

The cliffs at Tüchersfeld

Flower lady in Forchheim

across the valley toward Gössweinstein's **Castle** (*Burg Gössweinstein*), first mentioned in the 11th century and ultimately restored 100 years ago in a neo-Gothic style (daily Easter to October 10am–6pm).

From here, you can follow the river on the B470 past the towns of Muggendorf and Streitberg, both graced with castle ruins, or take a mountaintop shortcut through the farming village of Moggast: both routes lead through beautiful countryside to **Ebermannstadt**, which is known as the capital of the *Fränkische Schweiz*, and whose marketplace is surrounded by half-timbered houses. Make sure you see the old water wheel on the river Wiesent. About 13km (8 miles) further on is **Forchheim**, on the western border of the region. Forchheim saw its glory days from the 9th to 11th centuries, when it was a major centre for the Carolingian dynasty, the site of royal elections and parliamentary assemblies – although you'd never know it to look at the quiet little town it's become. Stop off to see its half-timbered houses and **Town Hall** dating from the 1500s. Don't miss the whimsical relief figures on the **Magistrate's Building** of 1535, including a self-portrait of its creator, Hans Ruhalm.

12. Nuremberg

From the Holy Roman Empire to the '1000 Year Reich', from its glowering round towers to Germany's great National Museum, Nuremberg brings history soberly, thoughtfully, excitingly to life.

The heavy damage **Nuremberg** sustained in World War II was not inflicted for any reason other than that this medieval city was a symbol of the German spirit, so much so that Hitler had chosen it to be the rallying grounds for his '1000-year empire': this is also why it was chosen by the Allies as the site for the post-war Nazi trials. Notwithstanding, Nuremberg – which has existed

Medieval Nuremberg

The Heilig-Geist-Spital on the Pegnitz

for more than 1000 years – does indeed represent some of what's finest about German culture. Today, carefully restored, Bavaria's second largest city has recovered its medieval air, complete with its skyline of round towers glowering above Gothic church spires, looking once again like the home of such artists of the Middle Ages and Renaissance as the poet Hans Sachs and the painter Albrecht Dürer.

Located on the A73 from Bamberg, the A3 from Würzburg, and the A9 from Munich, Nuremberg has so few places to park that you may want to consider arriving by train at the art nouveau railway station, which is an interesting sight in itself.

Enter the Old Town by way of Königsstrasse, past the threatening tower by **Königstor**, a reminder that city walls were originally designed to keep people out. Just inside the gateway to the left, you can see the **Handwerkerhof** (Artisans' Courtyard), a medieval-style tourist-oriented marketplace which actually dates from the 1970s.

The **Church of St Lawrence**, straight ahead of you up Königsstrasse, was constructed between the 13th and 15th centuries. Looking down the centre aisle, your eye is trapped in a kind of visual web: move closer to free your view from the wire grill between you and the beautiful, floating carving of the **Annunciation** by Veit Stoss. To the left and rear is an equally airy work: the soaring **Tabernacle** of Adam Kraft. *Kraft* means strength, and the name is illustrated by the self-portrait of Kraft at the bottom of the piece; chisel in hand, he's supporting the whole thing on his shoulders. Across from the cathedral is the tower of the **Nassau House**, Nuremberg's oldest private residence.

Crossing the river Pegnitz, you'll see the arches of the **Heilig-Geist-Spital** leading over the river on your right. Another of Bavaria's wonderful medieval homes for the aged and sick, still in use today, the facility was founded in 1332 with private funds; in the 16th century, it was built out over the river simply because there was no more space to expand it on land.

From the Spital, it's not far to the marketplace, where the broad facade of the **Frauenkirche** (Church of Our Lady) stands guard over the striped awnings of vendors or, in December, the original Bavarian *Christkindlmarkt* (Christmas market). This tradition dates from Nuremberg's conversion to Protestantism in 1525; when Luther did away with the Catholic canon of saints, he replaced the gift-giving days of St Nicholas Day (6 December) and Epiphany (6 January) with Christmas Eve, when the Christ Child (*Christkind*) brought gifts to all. It was actually the Nazis who revived the Christmas markets, but they've proved so enduringly popular that they've since spread through most of Catholic Bavaria, which ignores their Protestant roots in the interests of good business.

At one corner of the marketplace is the **Schöner Brunnen** (Beautiful Fountain), planned, like the rest of the square, under Emperor Charles IV; the fountain's forty figures range from Biblical prophets to King Arthur. Less attractive is the marketplace's history: it was built on the site of the Jewish quarter after it was levelled and its residents wiped out in 1349.

Rathausplatz runs between the 1340 **Rathaus** (Town Hall) and **St Sebald's**, one of Nuremberg's oldest churches, which contains the marvellous bronze **tomb of St Sebald** by Peter Vischer. To get from here to the **Burg**, or castle, which dominates the city, just walk toward the castle towers – uphill.

After around 1050, this castle kept Nuremberg an important centre for the Holy Roman Emperors for the next 500 years. Prominent here is the mighty **Sinwell Tower**; other features are the 50-m (164-ft) deep **Tiefer Brunnen** (Deep Well) and the double chapel, its upper level reserved for the Emperor and court, while the common people remained below (castle tours 9am–noon and 12.45–5pm, October to March 9.30am–noon and 12.45–4pm).

Walking down the street Am Ölberg from the castle will bring you to the square Beim Tiergärtnertor. Opposite half-timbered **Pilatus House** is the house where **Albrecht Dürer** lived for almost 20 years, today a small museum with furnished rooms and plenty of reproductions of Dürer's work (March to October and December Tuesday to Friday 10am–5pm, closed Monday; November, January and February Tuesday to Friday 1–5pm, Saturday and Sunday 10am–5pm). Albrecht-Dürer-Strasse is a quaint old street of shops and restaurants; stop off for lunch at number 6, the red-and-white

The Zeppelin Tribune

half-timbered **Albrecht Dürer Stube** (tel: 0911-227209).

Meander back through the city via **Weissgerbergasse** (one of Nuremberg's best-preserved old streets), down Maxplatz to the 15th-century house **Weinstadl**, then over the river at scenic **Maxbrücke**, from which you can see the oldest suspension bridge in Europe (1824). To the south, on Ludwigsplatz, the **Weißer Turm** (White Tower) is a remnant of the city's 13th-century fortifications; before it, the life-size figures on the modern fountain **Ehekarussell** represents a free interpretation of Hans Sachs's 16th-century poem about the ups and downs of marriage.

If you're in a museum-going mood, spend the rest of your day in the **Germanische Nationalmuseum** on nearby Kornmarkt. Founded in 1852 and devoted to the history, art, culture and daily life of the German-speaking world from 30,000BC to the present, it's one of the biggest and best museums in Europe. An afternoon is time enough to take in part of the art gallery, or the furniture or toy collection, or one of the museum's temporary exhibits (Tuesday to Sunday 10am–5pm, Wednesday until 9pm; English-language tours the first and third Sunday of each month).

If you'd rather miss the museum then take U-Bahn number 1 or 11 from the railway station one stop to Aufsessplatz and board tram 4 to Dutzendteich, at the edge of the **Nazi Rally Grounds** (*Reichsparteitagsgelände*), to see quite a different side of the city's past. Although the Nurembergers were not as a whole, in fact, very pro-Nazi in 1933, Hitler chose the city as the site for the annual Party Rally, and laid out the facilities on a typically grandiose scale. Many of the buildings have been left standing as a reminder of the past. Inside the **Zeppelin Tribune**, the exhibit **Faszination und Gewalt** ('Fascination and Power') explores the Nazi phenomenon (May to October Tuesday to Sunday 10am–6pm). There's also the Great Road, 60m (200ft) wide, and huge Congress Hall, never completed, by the Dutzendteich lake. The city has been at something of a loss to know what to do with some of these buildings; the grounds around them are, however, a lovely public park.

The castle at night

Lower Bavaria

Bavaria's two backwater provinces, the Upper Palatinate and Lower Bavaria (*Oberpfalz* and *Niederbayern*) are, in my opinion, two of its best. The country here includes the darkly beautiful Bavarian Forest, still with the feeling of wildness that more populous landscapes to the south have come to lack; while the cities – Regensburg, Passau and Landshut – haven't been fixed on the tourist map to the same degree as their westerly cousins. Travelling through the region means discovering hidden treasures. These provinces remain a well-kept secret; a visit here is highly recommended. The towns and cities can easily be reached by public transport, but for touring the Forest you are better off using a car.

Ferry across the Danube

Untouched by war and off the main tourist map, the ancient Free City and seat of Imperial Diets has kept not only its sense of the past, but the actual buildings themselves, from Roman remains to a medieval restaurant which has been serving sausage ever since the 12th century.

One of the few Bavarian cities spared in World War II, **Regensburg** wears its age with a flair distinct from that of rebuilt cities like Nuremberg, Würzburg or Augsburg. Perhaps this is precisely because it was never reconstructed: the builders of this city approached it without the preconceptions of modern restorers trained to revere and duplicate the past. Here, what you get is pure history and Regensburg's streets and buildings are somehow severe, sober testimony to the fact the people who once dwelt here were a race considerably different from soft modern man.

The Stone Bridge and the Cathedral

The city sprawls around the focal point of its **Cathedral**, and, if its lacy towers weren't built until the 1860s, the dark interior is clearly of another age. From the arching blackness, brilliant stained glass bursts forth with a luminosity unequalled in all but a handful of great Gothic cathedrals (Chartres comes to mind; and Bishop Leo was, in fact, inspired by French models in 1275, bringing in a French builder when his own workers, used to the Romanesque style, had trouble achieving the effect he wanted). Priceless medieval treasures, manufactured in the glassworks of Zwiesel and other towns, the windows float free of the dark walls and hover overhead with their vibrant, coloured light. Beneath them is the shine of the High Altar, made of silver and copper by Regensburg artisans in the 18th century. When your eyes have adjusted to the darkness, you can make out sculpture and carvings like the Annunciation Angel and Mary, standing opposite each other on the two front columns of the nave, the angel smiling in childish, Gothic delight. Adjacent to the church is little **All Saints' Chapel**, even older than the Cathedral, with the faded remains of its original, 12th-century frescoes.

Outside and toward the back of the building is the **Diocesan Museum of St Ulrich's**, a creatively renovated church containing Gothic art treasures from throughout Bavaria.

The Historische Wurstküche

Go along Altdorferplatz until you come to the Alter Kornmarkt, the city grain market from the Middle Ages to the 19th century, bordered by some of Regensburg's oldest buildings. Legend links the **Alte Kapelle** (Old Chapel), to the south, with Emperor Constantine and the year 313, as well as with Agilolfing dukes in the 700s; it's certain that Ludwig the German had it renovated for his palace in 875, although the building's baroque-ised interior doesn't betray any such advanced age. On the north side, by the arch you came through, the doughty **Roman Tower** was not, in fact, a product of the Romans, but of Carolingian builders topped (literally) by 13th-century craftsmen.

If it's old you want, go to the church called **Niedermünster** (on the street of the same name). It may seem like just any other baroque church, but excavations here uncovered traces of Roman and Germanic buildings dating back to the 2nd century (the Germanic tribes were wont to give the Romans a hard time, destroying their camp a couple of times in the 3rd century); in the 8th century, a church was built to house the tomb of St Erhard, to be replaced, in the 12th century, by the present building. Further on, the same street leads to Unter den Schwibbögen, where, to the left, you can clearly see remains of the **castle** (*Castra Regina*) which the Romans founded in 179 (replacing the impermanent little camps which had gone before), including the clumsy, massive arch of **Porta Pretoria**, the riverfront gate through the walls.

From here walk down to the bank of the Danube, where you can see the **Steinerne Brücke** (Stone Bridge) arching over the river. This bridge seemed a miracle when it was built in 1135, the first stone bridge in Europe. The story goes that the engineer in charge made a pact with the Devil in order to complete it, promising him the owners of the

Regensburg

240 m / 0.15 miles

Danube (Donau)
Kepler Str.
Fischmarkt
Old Town Hall
Ludwigstr.
Rathauspl.
Golden Tower
Gsandtenstr.
Am Öberg
Marschallstr.
Monastery
St Emmeram's Church
Helenenstr.
Palace
Albert Str.
Bahnhofstr.
Station
Stone Bridge
Historische Wurstküche
Thundorfer Str.
Eiserne Br.
Goliathstr.
Porta Pretoria
All Saints' Chapel
Niedermünster
Cathedral
Diocesan Museum of St Ulrich's
Roman Tower
Altdorferpl.
Alter Kornmarkt
Old Chapel
Residenzstr.
Obermünsterstr.
St.-Peters-Weg
Fröhliche Türkenstr.
Maximilianstr.
Luther- Str.
D.-Martin-
Rote-Hahnen-Str.
Untere
Bachgasse

The Romans left their mark

first eight legs across the bridge, and then foiling him by sending over a dog and two chickens. Before the bridge, built into the old city walls, is the modest **Historische Wurstküche** (Tel: 0941-59098), a Regensburg trademark, which allegedly began serving up its delicious, low-priced sausages for workers on the bridge in the 12th century.

Brückstrasse runs back into the city and to Goliathstrasse, where the **Goliath House** features a gigantic mural of David and Goliath, a kind of ornament common in the 16th century. As you walk down this street, you can see the tall **Golden Tower**, a 13th-century house, on Wahlenstrasse to your left. Just before you come to Rathausplatz, you'll see the old corner building which houses the mini-restaurant **Dampfnudel-Ulli** (Watmarkt 4, tel: 0941-53297), an ideal place to sample the ultra-Bavarian speciality *Dampfnudel*.

Fronting Rathausplatz is the **Altes Rathaus** (Old Town Hall), medieval in aspect, complete with drunkenly leaning walls and sloping stairs. Buy tickets in the tourist office on the ground floor for tours of the **Reichstagsmuseum** (English tours May to September, Monday to Saturday at 3.15pm), where you can see everything from council to torture chambers and learn quite a bit about the history of this city-state, which hosted Imperial Diets, or councils (Reichstag), from the 1600s to the 1800s.

From here, walk down Untere Bachgasse to **St Emmeram's Church**. Yet another claimant to the title of 'Oldest Church in Regensburg', St Emmeram's was formerly a monastery which in the early Middle Ages was the most important in Bavaria. Begun in the 8th century, it reflects changing architectural tastes through the ages, notably the cloisters (11th–14th centuries) and a baroque interior by the Asam brothers.

When secularisation closed the monasteries in 1806, the adjoining *Kloster* came into the possession of the Counts of Thurn und Taxis, an aristocratic family which made its fortune with a monopoly on the postal service dating back to the 16th century. As soon as they obtained it, the Princes set about turning the monastery into a magnificent palace, which, still inhabited, is open for tours (April to October daily 11am, 2, 3 and 4pm, additional tours Saturday, Sunday and holidays 10am; November to March weekends and holidays only at 10 and 11am and 2 and 3pm).

Danube illuminations

Watch vases being blown by the glassmakers of Zwiesel; then drive through the countryside of the Bavarian Forest to one of the loveliest places in Germany, the 'three-river city' of Passau.

Between Regensburg and Passau, the meandering Danube river (Donau) forms the southern border of one of Bavaria's less-known wonders: the **Bavarian Forest** (*Bayerischer Wald*). Lying between the Danube and the Czech border, this mountainous region is still off the beaten track – in part because its landscapes, which would be a major attraction in any other country, are overshadowed, in Bavaria, by the Alps. The area has thus remained the province of German holiday-makers who know a good thing in their own country when they see it.

Deep in the forest

The little town of **Zwiesel** (*Autobahn* from Regensburg to Deggendorf, then north on the B11 via Regen) lies only a few kilometres from the border of the Czech Republic. And it isn't only landscape which the region has in common with Czech Bohemia. Minerals in the soil are partly responsible for the fame of Bohemian glass throughout the world, and the drawing of a border didn't prevent the glassmaker's art from flourishing wherever this fertile ground was to be found.

Most of Zwiesel's innumerable **glass workshops** offer tours of the premises, allowing you to watch the painstaking processes by which glass is blown, cut, and even painted with delicate floral designs. Although tours are given only at fixed times, each manufacturer has an outlet which observes normal business hours (usually 9am–6pm, Saturday until 2pm); some of these are even open on Sunday, quite a rarity in Germany.

The workshops of **Ambiente** (Frauenauer Strasse 110; left off the ring road around the town, then left again) retain a rustic air, and the glassware they produce has a distinctive hand-blown quality (you can watch glassmakers at work Monday to Friday 10am–4pm, Saturday until 1pm). An equally rustic product is to be found at the nearby **Bärwurzerei Hieke** distillery, Frauenauerstrasse 82 (for guided tours call 09922-1515). *Bärwurz* is the signature *digestif* of the Bavarian Forest, distilled from a special blend of local herbs; the tasting session offered on these premises should separate *Bärwurz* fans from foes.

Continue up the ring road to **Theresienthal**, where you can see the

A glassmaker plies his trade

more polished, packed-for-export products of **Schott** glassworks, or visit the **Theresienthal** glass workshop next door (half-hour tours Tuesday to Thursday 9.30am–1pm; Monday and Friday 9.30–11.30am; Saturday (summer months only) 9.30am–1pm). The complex of buildings in Theresienthal also includes the **Glass Museum** (10am–2pm) and **Theresienhof** (tel: 09922-60530), a rustic restaurant with regional dishes. Outdoor types can pick up tips from the **National Park's Information Centre**, also here.

From Zwiesel, take roads to Frauenau and Grafenau. With the sharp green of the meadows framed by sombre-toned evergreens, the landscapes here, particularly on a misty day, retain the feeling of the Old Germany depicted in fairy tales and storybooks. **Grafenau** is the centre of the **Bavarian Forest National Park**. Stop here if you have time, and follow the trails of the wild animal preserve, a sanctuary for bears, European bison, lynxes and wild boar. From Grafenau, the B85 leads down to the Danube (Donau); suddenly, you're driving along a road with cliffs above you, a river below, and, over the bridge ahead of you to your right, the other-worldly, truly enchanting city of Passau.

Sitting on today's Austrian border in a far corner of Germany, **Passau** was a stronghold and urban centre for Celtic, Roman and medieval civilisations. An independent principality from 1217–1803, and a major force in the Holy Roman Empire of the 13th century,

An aerial view of Passau

Typical 'Tracht'

its power waned in the shadow of Austro-Hungary, and Napoleon, finally, appended it to Bavaria. At the confluence of three rivers, it at least managed to maintain economic importance as a shipping centre: goods from the Inn river were loaded onto Danube barges to travel to Vienna or Budapest. Today, although the Rhine-Main-Danube canal, a massive project undertaken in 1921 to link the North Sea to the Black and finally opened in the autumn of 1992, may mean a revival of shipping trade, the main water traffic around Passau is passenger ships loaded with sightseers. Politically, the town is renowned as a bastion of arch-conservatism, as illustrated by the film *The Nasty Girl* (*Das Schreckliche Mädchen*), which delves into the local Nazi past. Nonetheless, it's a sleepy, watery, magical town, Germany's answer to Venice with its old houses (the buildings with the wilted air of fading roses), baroque architecture, and the brightness, even on grey days, that comes from light reflected off broad surfaces of water.

Built on a narrow spit of land, the small city is ideally suited for pedestrians; leave your car in one of the car parks (there are several near the bridge from the B85) before walking along the Danube and up Rindermarkt. To the right, Luragogasse leads to Domplatz and **St Stephen's Cathedral**. Passau, seat of the bishopric since 789, saw churches on this site in the days of the Romans; today's baroque cathedral was built when an earlier, Gothic building burned in the city fire of 1662. Huge and solid, ornate with white stucco figures like icing on a wedding cake, the building houses the largest organ in the world, with more than 17,000 pipes. Noon concerts are given on weekdays from May to October.

The largest organ in the world

Behind the Cathedral is the 18th-century **Bishop's Residence**. A left turn on Schrottgasse brings you back to the Danube. On your left is the hotel **Wilder Mann** (tel: 0851-35071), with a reputable fifth-floor restaurant; and on your right is the **Town Hall**, its painted facade sporting some delightful stone carvings and a line indicating the heights of flood waters from the 16th century to the 20th. From here, you should take the shuttle bus that runs half-hourly (11.30am–5pm from April to October, except Monday, Friday until 7pm) to the hilltop castle **Veste Oberhaus** across the river. The castle (Tuesday to Sunday 9am–5pm, closed February) has proved itself many times as a defensive outpost since it was begun in 1219; Napoleon even used it in 1805. Inside, the **City Museum** displays armour and costumes, a smithy, and a 14th-century chapel, while there's an impressive view of the city and rivers below.

Walking along the Danube towards the end of the Passau peninsula, you'll pass row upon row of tour boats offering a range of cruises – everything from the scenic cliffs of the Donaudurchbruch (Danube Gap) near Regensburg to longer jaunts down-river to Vienna. From the tip of the peninsula, dubbed **Three-River Corner** (*Dreiflußeck*), you have a view of all of Passau's rivers: on your left, the narrow Ilz emerges from the Bavarian Forest to meet the Danube; on your right, the Inn leads up from the south. Each of the rivers is a different colour, and the Inn's chalky and the Ilz's dark waters contrast with those of the green, beautiful not-so-blue Danube.

From the Inn Promenade, a pedestrian bridge (past the road bridge) leads left over the river to **St Severin's church**. Severin saw this church built before he died in 482; it was expanded in the 10th century, and reno-vated in 1497. Its white interior has the cleanness of old bones, speaking of a past so distant it's hard to comprehend.

Passau from the river

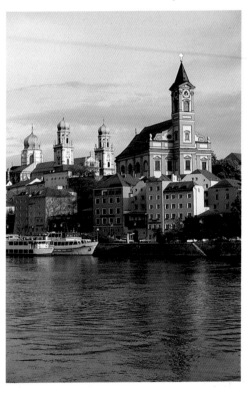

Leaving the church and passing under an arch in the medieval town wall, follow Am Severinstor to the **Roman Museum** (March–November Tuesday–Sunday 10am–noon and 2–4pm), located on the site where excavators uncovered remains of the Roman castle *Boiotro*. The Romans' bridge across the Inn was near here; today, you'll have to use the pedestrian bridge to return to the city centre and the restaurants Wilder Mann mentioned earlier or **Weisser Hase** (Ludwig-strasse 23, tel: 0851-92110) for dinner.

Along the Danube to Osterhofen and one of Bavaria's hidden baroque treasures. On to the river city of Landshut, capital of Lower Bavaria, with its brick Cathedral, castle, and ducal residence in German and Italian style.

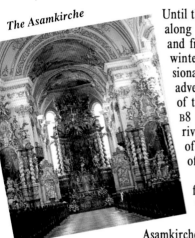

The Asamkirche

Until the beginning of the 1980s, the narrow B8 along the Danube was the only access road to and from Passau – and what with ice in the winter, constant heavy traffic, and the occasional flood, it wasn't much fun to drive. The advent of the *Autobahn* along the other side of the river changed all that, and now the B8 can be seen for what it is: a pleasant riverside road through the pastel-lit scenery of the Danube valley, with the blue hills of the Bavarian Forest in the distance.

After about three-quarters of an hour from Passau, you'll get to **Osterhofen**: turn left at the traffic light toward Altenmarkt, and follow signs to the Asamkirche. Here, in the heart of Lower Bavaria, is one of the Asam brothers' greatest masterpieces: **St Margarethe**. Elaborate baroque flourishes and frescoes are so well harmonised that the church seems, quite simply, a spectacular whole. Its location also sets it off: that a farming community matter-of-factly attends Mass in this museum piece of a building illustrates the way Bavaria's artistic heritage is kept vividly, even startlingly, alive.

Continue on the B8 to Plattling, then follow signs to Wallersdorf and get on the B11 along the river Isar to **Landshut**. The skyline is recognisable by two towers: Trausnitz Castle, perched on a rise over the town, and the spire of St Martin's Cathedral, the tallest brick tower in the world at 131m (430ft). Drive right through town (left at the railway station down Luitpoldstrasse, and over the river) and park by the Isar in the big car park off Wittstrasse, from which it's only a short walk to the city centre.

Founded in 1204, a Wittelsbach capital on and off for the ensuing centuries, and now capital of Lower Bavaria, Landshut presents much of the aspect of a busy old market town which it must have displayed in the 1600s. Its main street, **Altstadt** (Old Town), is essentially a wide square surrounded with the kind of gabled houses familiar from Northern Renaissance painting; yet, filled with the hustle and bustle of modern life (shoppers hunting bargains, young people hanging out in front of McDonalds), it seems successfully to have made the transition to the present, rather than remaining tied, museum-like, to its past.

The most striking monument on this street is, of course, **St Martin's Cathedral** and its aforementioned tower, all built entirely of

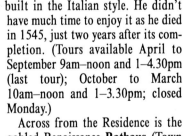

brick. Inside and out, brightly painted terracotta figures ornament portals and pillars; more recent stained glass includes, in the right aisle, a depiction of the **Landshuter Hochzeit**, the famous wedding that took place in 1475 between George, the son of Duke Ludwig the Rich, and the Polish king's daughter, Jadwiga.

The event is an integral part of local history, celebrated in an enormous July pageant every four years. The far left-hand panel of the detailed sandstone altar depicts St Martin dividing his cloak to give to the beggar. Another interesting carving is on the south side of the church: a portrait of sculptor Hans von Burghausen (also called Stethaimer), builder of this and as many as 50 other churches in the area, who died in 1432.

Cross Altstadt to come to Landgasse and the **Vitztumb**, a building that served as Residence to the three last Dukes of Lower Bavaria (Ludwig the Rich, fat and gouty, died here in 1479), and later contained administrative offices.

But this old building wasn't enough for Ludwig X. Second son of Duke Albrecht IV, the man who instituted the law of primogeniture, Ludwig insisted that, as the law was passed after his birth, he still had the right to half the duchy of Bavaria; accordingly, he governed in Landshut while big brother Wilhelm reigned in Munich. Nor was Trausnitz Castle up to Ludwig's standards; city residences were all the rage in the 1500s, and he accordingly started his own **Residenz** on Altstadt in 1530. The typical German palace facing the street is joined to a very Italianate arcade and wing; a trip to the court of Mantua in 1537 so inspired Ludwig that he had the rest of his Residence built in the Italian style. He didn't

have much time to enjoy it as he died in 1545, just two years after its completion. (Tours available April to September 9am–noon and 1–4.30pm (last tour); October to March 10am–noon and 1–3.30pm; closed Monday.)

Across from the Residence is the gabled Renaissance **Rathaus** (Town Hall); inside, frescoes depict the famous wedding. Further down the street, Altstadt 362 belongs to one of Landshut's breweries, Koller-Fleischmann, and houses both the comfortable **Café Woch'nblatt** and the disco **Bauhaus** (open after 9pm).

A juxtaposition of styles

The mighty Trausnitz Castle

Follow Rosengasse right from Altstadt to **Neustadt**; the 'new' in this broad street's name is somewhat misleading, as it was laid out in 1300. From here, Regierungsstrasse leads off to the former **Dominican monastery** which has housed the government (*Regierung*) of Lower Bavaria since 1839; adjacent to this is the green facade of a rococo church. Before you reach the building, Kramergasse, on the right, leads to the rectangular square **Freyung** dominated by the towers of **St Jodok** at one end. This square is the site of seasonal open-air markets such as the ceramics market; Landshut is, in fact, a centre for this craft, with one of Bavaria's only ceramics schools.

From Freyung, follow Kolpingstrasse to the **Hofgarten** (Court Garden), one of Bavaria's oldest and largest, its footpaths leading to scenic overlooks of the city on the way to **Burg Trausnitz** (Trausnitz Castle), an occasional residence of Wittelsbach dukes since 1204, expanded and reworked over the years (Duke Wilhelm IV followed Uncle Ludwig's penchant for the Italian Renaissance in his alterations of 1568), and, after all that, damaged heavily by fire in 1961. You can still see **St George's Chapel** and the distinctive **Narrentreppe** ('Fools' Staircase'), frescoed in 1578 with huge Commedia dell'Arte figures; perhaps even better is the view over the city from the castle's high balcony. When you descend from the heights, wander along the river, where the city's old buildings are reflected in the water and cafés and eateries like **Isar Klause** (tel: 0871-23100) fill with relaxed drinkers and diners as night falls.

Down by the river

Shopping

Mention Bavaria and many non-Germans will immediately think of *Lederhosen*, hats with 'shaving brushes' (usually made out of a tuft of chamois hair) and beer mugs. It's true that these items are readily available in the shops – and at far higher prices than one might have expected – but the discriminating shopper, whether hunting for an inexpensive souvenir or a valuable memento, will be able to find more distinctive, individual Bavarian objects. And shopping in Bavaria certainly isn't limited to local handicrafts. Cities like Munich offer a full range of international, cosmopolitan fashions, in clothing, furniture, books, and what-have-you.

Folk Crafts

Tracht, the folkloric costumes sported by locals at Oktoberfest or village fairs, is more than just a quaint affectation, as the unwitting shopper will be quick to discover from the pricetags on the *Lederhosen* or *Dirndl* (dress) of choice. These outfits signal the region from which the wearer hails; and people who see their folk outfit as a reflection of their cultural heritage and identity are more than willing to pay for the skilled hand labour that goes into assembling one of these complicated ensembles.

Those who don't want a complete outfit can still invest in one of the *Tracht* accessories, such as a hat or fringed shawl. Munich's **Loden-Frey** (Maffeistrasse 7–9) and **Wallach** (Residenzstrasse 3), both in the city centre, are two of that city's finest outlets; Wallach also offers a range of Bavarian handicrafts. Sometimes you can find cheap *Tracht* in secondhand shops; there's a concentration of these on and around Occamstrasse in Schwabing.

Another major artisan industry is carved wood, a particular speciality of Upper Bavaria. From simple cutting boards to painted Madonnas and detailed Nativity scenes, you'll find it in

Pottery for sale

Wood carvings come in all shapes and sizes

the *Holzschnitzereien* (woodcarvers) and *Holzläden* (wood shops) of Munich and the Alpine foothills. Oberammergau is a notable centre for the craft: its streets are lined with shop windows filled with assemblages of carved and painted figures. In some rural shops, such as the *Holzschnitzerei* on Linderhoferstrasse 29, in Graswang, you may be able to see the master carvers at work; on the other hand, city shops, such as Munich's **Leute Holzwaren** (Viktualienmarkt 15), tend to have wider selections, including functional, not merely decorative, wooden items. In December, Munich or Nuremberg are the places to be if you're shopping for a Nativity scene: artisans come to the Christmas markets from all over Bavaria. Although complete scenes are expensive, individual figures can also be purchased.

Pewter (*Zinn*) objects – candlesticks and Christmas ornaments, serving dishes and soldiers – are sold at *Zinngiessereien* all over Bavaria; for a sampling, look in at **Mory Zinngiesserei** in the Munich Town Hall building, or **Antonie Kaiser**, behind the church of St Peter. In Passau, **Bauernkammel** (Steinweg 2) offers a variety of trinkets, most of them pewter. Bavarian ceramics also have a distinctive look: a ceramic 'bread pot' (*Brottopf*), rather than a bread box, can be found in nearly every Bavarian home. Landshut is home to an official school of ceramics; every September, the city hosts a three-day market, the **Haferlmarkt**, which attracts dozens of exhibitors. In Munich, the **Münchner Puppenstube** (Maxburgstrasse 4), which has a range of local crafts, carries a nice selection of ceramics. Available in ceramic, pewter or glass are the traditional beer mugs, called *Masskrug* in German.

An optical display

Folk crafts are also sold in departments of the major retail outlets of most Bavarian cities. Most Bavarian – indeed, German – cities have a branch of **Hertie**, **Karstadt**, or **Kaufhof**, which sell everything from *Tracht* to *Mode* (fashion), electronics (*Elektrogeräte*) to pantyhose (*Strumpf*). If it's German high fashion you want, there are always Margarethe Ley's **Escada** and **Laurèl**, **Wolfgang Joop**, and **Jil Sander**, with outlets in many cities. A famous Munich eccentric is the men's fashion designer **Rudolph Moshammer**, whose shop is at Maximilianstrasse 14. Of more general interest is Munich's landmark department store **Ludwig Beck am Rathauseck**, on Marienplatz, which has designer fashions, Bavarian specialities, and, at Christmastime, in-house artisans working on their crafts. Also in Munich is **Radspieler**, at Hackenstrasse 4 and 7, which is crammed with an eclectic mix of art supplies, kitchenware, leather goods, and clothing.

Glass and China

Serious collectors and brides-to-be should head for the Bavarian Forest to stock up on their table settings and trousseau. Zwiesel and the surrounding area is filled with glass retail outlets (*see Day 14*), while the Upper Palatinate (Oberpfalz) to the north and east is rife with factory outlets selling name-brand goods at very good prices. About 45km (28 miles) north of Regensburg, the towns of Weiden and Neustadt an der Waldnaab contain legion crystal factory outlets, such as **Nachtmann Bleikristall** (lead crystal) (Tel: 09602-30176) and **Glas von Marion** (tel: 09602-7462), both in Neustadt. Farther north, in Mitterteich, is the **Mitterteich Porcelain Factory Outlet** (tel: 09633-300). More central is Munich's **Nymphenburg Porcelain** factory, with showrooms in the Northern Schloss Rondell at Nymphenburg Palace and a store on Odeonsplatz.

Wines, Liqueurs and Delicatessen

It may be a bit much to ship home a crate of Bavarian beer, but a bottle of Franconian wine isn't difficult to transport. Famous for its dry white wines, Würzburg has plenty of purveyors of the local vintages, such as the Spitals or the **Haus des Frankenweins** on the river Main. Many parts of Bavaria have typical liqueurs which also make unusual souvenirs. In the Bavarian Forest, it's *Bärwurz*; the Alps have *Enzian*, made from gentian root. Some monasteries and convents, like **Kloster Ettal** or **Frauenchiemsee**, continue to distill their own blends.

In Munich there is a choice of delicatessens. Situated behind the Town Hall, **Dallmayr** is a temple of fine food; while **Feinkost Käfer** has its own building on Prinzregentenstrasse, a whole department store of food.

Carnival masks from the baker

Eating Out

Bavarian cuisine is either hearty or heavy, depending on your appetite and your mood. Main dishes are almost without exception based on pork, potato, and cabbage products; other vegetables are rare. To a traveller, the advantage of this kind of rustic cuisine is that you can discover marvellous meals in a tiny village *Lokal*: in Bavaria, good cooking is not the province of cities. There is also the choice offered by international restaurants – mostly Greek and Italian – even in the smallest of country towns.

A hallmark of the Bavarian diet is sausage (*Wurst*), displayed in the windows of butchers' shops (*Metzgereien*) in a mind-boggling range of sizes and varieties (a Berchtesgaden butcher even advertises *Touristenwurst*; one only hopes, in the town's summer crowds, that this is sausage *for* tourists, not, as the name might suggest, made of). Munich's particular speciality is *Weisswurst*, a light, white veal sausage flecked with parsley. A veritable religion has sprung up around these: they must be simmered, never boiled; served in a tureen of hot water; peeled before eating; dolloped with a particular kind of dark, sweet, grainy mustard (many restaurants have their own recipes) – and all this at mid-morning, the traditional time for the 'Weisswurst break'. Regardless of the early hour, the only possible beverage to accompany this snack is beer – *Weissbier* (a cloudy, yeasty brew with a distinctive flavour) at that.

Long red and brown *Bratwürste* (fried sausage) are common throughout the German-speaking world; but another distinctly Bavarian variety is the small, delicious, *Nürnberger Bratwurst*, usually served in sixes on a bed of *Sauerkraut*. In Franconia the sausages of choice are *Blaue Zipfel*, thin, tangy sausages in a vinegary brine, named for their slightly bluish grey hue. On the dinner table, *Wurst* only appear in groups; a *Wurstteller* (platter) will include several different varieties. Don't confuse this with a *Schlachtteller* ('slaughter platter'), which is an arrangement of fresh blood and liver sausage together with pieces of boiled pork and kidney.

Another speciality is the ubiquitous *Leberkäse* (literally, 'liver-cheese'), a bologna-like meat loaf which languishes under heat lamps

Schweinebraten mit Semmelknödel

in every snack bar (*Imbissstube*) in Upper Bavaria; slabs of it are smeared with mustard and served in a *Semmel* (roll) for eaters on the go. However, when homemade in a country butcher's, fried on both sides and served with fried eggs and potatoes, it can be very tasty indeed. Mention should also be made of the distinctive Upper Bavarian *Saure Lüngerl*, sliced lung prepared in a special vinegar sauce.

A stand-by of every Bavarian restaurant is *Schweinebraten mit Blaukraut und Knödel* – roast pork with red cabbage and dumpling.

Dumplings come in two varieties: *Semmelknödel*, made of rolls, and *Kartoffelknödel*, made of grated potatoes. For real pork fans, *Schweinshax'n* – pork knuckles – are as Bavarian as it gets. Repellent to some, delicious to others, they arrive encased in an armour of crisp skin and bubbling fat.

There are also options for non-meat eaters. *Rahmchampignons* (or *Pilze*) *mit Semmelknödel* are mushrooms in a cream sauce poured over a huge dumpling, which make a filling meal. Imported from Baden in the west and taken over by the Swabians, *Kässpätzle* can be found on most menus: this is a kind of homemade pasta with melted cheese and onion.

Beer gardens have their own specialities. You'll find *Hax'n* aplenty, as well as roast chicken (*Hendl*); *Rippchen*, spare ribs, are also popular. Giant pretzels (*Brez'n*) are a treat; if you want to be really Bavarian, smear them with *Obazda*, an orangey cheese spread made with camembert, butter, paprika and onion. You may notice people eating something that looks like paper: these are *Radi*, thinly sliced white radishes. To enjoy these properly, salt them and let them sit a few minutes until the salt is absorbed.

Beer, of course, is a favourite beverage; but you have to decide whether you want blond beer (*Helles*) or dark (*Dunkles*), yeasty, wheaty *Weissbier*, or even *dunkles Weissbier*. Then there's *Starkbier* in March, and *Wiesnbier* at the Oktoberfest, and, in Bamberg, *Rauchbier*... After all this, you may want to settle for *alkoholfreies Bier*, that is if you don't opt for the local shandy known as *Radler* (named after the Bavarian word for cyclist). If you don't drink beer at all, the only way to get a decent amount of liquid in a restaurant is to order a *Spezi* (half cola, half orange soda) or an *Apfelschorle* (half apple juice, half mineral water).

The word *Restaurant* works in most languages, but you may not find one of these in a small town: the word in German denotes something a bit more upmarket than it does in English. The general term for eateries is *Gaststätten*: this covers everything from fine dining to the corner pub (*Kneipe*, or *Lokal*). *Konditoreien* serve cake and coffee, as well, sometimes, as light meals; for *Wurst* and sandwiches, there's the corner *Schnellimbiss* (snack bar).

Munich

WEISSES BRÄUHAUS
Im Tal 7
Tel: 089-299875
A venerable establishment whose decor is as authentically Bavarian as the *Schweinshax'n* and *Knödel* it serves. True Münchners come here at 11am to eat *Weisswurst*, a speciality of the city. Visitors should treat the strong dark *Weissbier* with respect.

GEORGENHOF
Friedrichstrasse 1
Tel: 393101
Bavarian dining with a touch of class, in an ambience that manages to be both rustic and slightly elegant. Where I take out-of-town guests.

Füssen

ZUM SCHWANEN
Brotmarkt 4
Tel: 08362-6174
Located in a building dating from the 15th century and serving elegant, yet still very Bavarian, cuisine (the changing daily menu is well worth sampling).

Oberammergau

GRÖBL-ALM
On the B23 between Linderhof and Graswang
Tel: 08822-6434
A fine place to go for a hearty Bavarian lunch while looking down over

Weisswurst is eaten in the morning

Lunchtim

the green valley and the Alps. Meal include venison (*Wild*) with cranber ries (*Preiselbeeren*), which in goo weather can be eaten at one of th shaded tables on the outdoor terrac

EIBSEE HOTEL
On Lake Eibsee
Tel: 08821-98810
With its lakeside balcony commandin a marvellous view of the Zugspitz this restaurant offers fine dining. Th cuisine reflects a French influence (wi corresponding prices), although th menu includes the requisite Bavaria *Wurst* and cheese, spruced up a litt to match the surroundings. The fre grilled trout (*Forelle*) is delicious.

Mittenwald

ALPENROSE
Obermarkt 1
Tel: 08823-92700
One of Mittenwald's oldest, and mo atmospheric, restaurants. Try som thing traditional like liver dumpli soup (*Leberknödelsuppe*) followed Schweinebraten mit Blaukraut or, you want something lighter, a plate *Käsespätzle*. Live music some evening

Chiemsee

GASTHOF INSELWIRT
Frauenchiemsee
Tel: 08054-630
A traditional eatery with a large te race overlooking the water that ten to be crowded with *Wurst-* a *Schwein*-hungry visitors.

Berchtesgaden

OTEL-GASTHOF NUTZKASER
*ust off the B305 from Berchtesgaden to
amsau (signs to Hochschwarzeck)*
el: 08657-388

family-run establishment perched on
steep hillside, where you can eat your
l of hearty Bavarian fare in full sight
the Alps.

Augsburg

JGGEREI-STUBE
koberstrasse 26
el: 0821-30870

ecialities include a plate of *Wurst*,
ahmchampignons mit Semmelknödel
d a selection of local Augsburg
ers.

JNIG VON FLANDERN BRAUEREI
arolinenstrasse 12
el: 0821-158050

increasingly popular basement
ng-out which serves varieties of its
vn in-house brew, as well as light
eals and snacks.

Dinkelsbühl

EISSES ROSS
eingasse 12
l: 09851-2274

is acclaimed restaurant is sometimes
oked for businessmen attending sem-
ars and conferences. Its updated ver-
ns of a variety of traditional dishes
well worth sampling.

Rothenburg

OTEL REICHS-KÜCHENMEISTER
rchplatz 8-10
l: 09861-9700

pleasant place to stop, offering all
standard German dishes to a pre-
minantly tourist clientele.

OTEL GOLDENER HIRSCH
tere Schmiedgasse 16-25
l: 09861-7080

is restaurant is a little too well-

known for its own good, but offers
meals that are a cut above most tourist
fare, even if a bit pricey. There are a
variety of dining areas, including an
outdoor terrace with a lovely view of
the town.

Würzburg

BÜRGERSPITAL WEINSTUBEN
Theaterstrasse 19
Tel: 0931-352880
Sample a local wine, perhaps together
with *Weinblatz*, a kind of thick spiced
poppadum, or *Weinbeisser* (a long,
thin cured sausage).

ZUM STACHEL
Gressengasse 1
Tel: 0931-52770
A venerable establishment dating back
to 1413. It is rife with history (and
flowers).

Bamberg

BRUDERMÜHLE
Schranne 1
Tel: 0951-955220
The restaurant has attracted national
attention for its fine cuisine A good
place to come for a special occasion
– prices are not cheap.

SCHLENKERLA
Dominikanerstrasse 6
Tel: 0951-56060
This traditional Bamberg restaurant,
located in a 14th-century house, has
been brewing – or smoking – its own
beer since 1678. Closed Tuesday.

An Upper Bavarian institution

Bucolic balconies

Pegnitz

PFLAUMS POSTHOTEL PEGNITZ
Nürnbergerstrasse 12-16
Tel: 09241-7250
One of the preeminent German restaurants, it serves world-class meals at world-class prices; although the adjacent Posthalterstube has a menu of local specialities for those on a slightly tighter budget.

Nuremberg

ALBRECHT DÜRER STUBE
Albrecht-Dürer-Strasse 6
Tel: 0911-227209
This half-timbered house provides a perfect setting in which to try the delicious *Nürnberger Bratwurst*.

Regensburg

HISTORISCHE WURSTKÜCHE
Adjacent to Stone Bridge
(Steinerne Brücke)
Tel: 0941-59098
Tucked into a section of the original city wall, the small kitchen serves tourists and locals, either in the smoky interior or at outdoor tables on the bank of the Danube; a visit to Regensburg isn't complete without a stop-off here.

BISCHOFSHOF
Krauterermarkt 3
Tel: 0941-59086
Hotel restaurant trusted for good local specialities, from *Schwein* to Strudel.

Try some Saure Lüngerl

Passau

WILDER MANN
Am Rathausplatz
Tel: 0851-35071
One of Passau's oldest restaurants the fifth floor of the hotel.

WEISSER HASE
Ludwigstrasse 23
Tel: 0851-92110
While not enjoying quite the same re utation as Wilder Mann for fine fa this establishment serves reliable lo cuisine at more moderate prices.

Landshut

HERZOGSTÜBERL
(in Hotel Fürstenhof)
Stethaimer Strasse 3
Tel: 0871-92550
A high-quality menu of up-scale reg nal specialities with a French touc

ISAR KLAUSE
Laendstrasse 124 (in summer acc from the river)
Tel: 0871-23100
Situated on the Isar this is a go place to sample wine and *Wurst*, other dishes at affordable prices.

84

Nightlife

The term 'nightlife' covers a multitude of evils — particularly in Bavaria, where the population is divided between those who want to play all night and those who'd rather just go to bed. Although early closing laws hamper night owls in many areas — this isn't Berlin, where places stay open all night — anyone who wants an evening on the town shouldn't have any problem dancing into the wee hours of the morning in cities like Munich or Würzburg. The large number of concert halls and theatres, meanwhile, makes you remember that Germany was one of the great cradles of Western music; classical music lovers will be in hog heaven.

Dance Fever

Munich discos often close at three or four in the morning; popular venues include the enormous **Park Cafe** (Sophienstrasse 7, tel: 089-598313), jet-setting **P1** (for the older, richer set, in the Haus der Kunst at Prinzregentenstrasse 1, tel: 089-294252), and **Nachtwerk** (Landsberger Strasse 185, tel: 089-5704344), increasingly a venue for good live bands from around the world. In the heart of Schwabing, **Occamstrasse** is lined with a variety of clubs, bars, and discos. Trendy **Nacht Cafe** (Maximilianplatz 5, tel: 089-595900) is a place

A bar in Munich's Schwabing

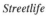

to go to hear live music but not necessarily to dance; it's open until 5am (and you can also eat there). By this time **Schmalznudel**, at the Viktualienmarkt, has also opened its doors; open only 5am–2pm, this German equivalent of a doughnut shop is the place in Munich to wind down a long. night.

In Würzburg, **Sanderstrasse** has a range of pubs (like **Robert's Bar**, Sanderstrasse 76, tel: 0931-16868); you can also dance at **Café Ludwig**, near the train station (Kaiserstrasse 5, tel: 0931-51522). Nuremberg's disco **Das Boot** is that city's popular dance venue; people also hang out at the café **Ruhestörung**, or, in summer, on **Albrecht-Dürer-Platz**, carpeted with young people singing, playing guitars, or just talking. In Regensburg, **Skala** is the disco of choice; but fans of ballroom dancing young and old can also go to Tanz Café. Landshut offers, in addition to the disco **Brauhaus** (*see itinerary 15*), the newly renovated **Amadeus** (Isargestade 727, tel: 0871-22604).

Munich, Augsburg, Würzburg, and Nuremberg, in particular, have become more or less regular stops on the European tours of major pop stars and groups, from Michael Jackson to Metallica. One place to get tickets is at the ticket window in the underground station of Munich's Marienplatz (Tel: 089-264620), where you can also pick up schedules and tickets for other cities.

Another choice for the evening

Garmisch, which has something of a reputation as a playboys' (or rich ski bums') haunt in any case, is one of the few Bavarian towns with a **gambling casino** (Am Kurpark 10, tel: 08821-53099, daily from 3pm).

Classical Concerts

Of the fifteen itineraries in this book, over half describe places with their own municipal theatres, staging opera and operetta as well as spoken drama (and sometimes exclusively the former) – an indication of just how important old-fashioned art forms like opera are to the man on the street in Europe. In smaller towns, there won't be a performance every night; your best bet is to check schedules at the tourist information office to see what's on when you get to town.

Opera houses are closed in July and August, but to compensate, there are summer festivals in Munich and Bayreuth (Munich's **Opernfestspiel** is held in July; Bayreuth's Wagner-only **Festspiel** in August). Tickets, alas, are very difficult to come by, especially in Bayreuth, where it is common for people to spend years on waiting lists before being admitted into the inner sanctum. In Munich, however, you can now order tickets for the National Theater by phone and pay by credit card (tel: 089-21851920).

If all else fails, go to the theatre before the performance and look hopeful; you may come across someone selling a ticket (*Karte*). It's easier to gain access to the open-air summer performances at the amphitheatre by the **Roter Tor** in Augsburg.

The state of orchestral music in Germany is just as robust as opera: Munich alone, for example, boasts four major orchestras. The Munich Philharmonic plays in the modern *Philharmonie*, one of four concert halls in the modern Gasteig Culture Centre; the Bayerischer Rundfunk (Bavarian Radio) orchestra also appears in the Herkulessaal.

Bamberg is also anchored on the international music map; its world-class orchestra has recently acquired its own concert hall. All this concert activity continues in summer, which sees various festivals such as Würzburg's **Mozart Festival** in June, featuring great musicians playing in the gardens of the Residence. Garmisch, in July, celebrates the work of local boy Richard Strauss.

Other Pursuits

Of course, in Bavaria there are legion other things to do at night, from spending an evening in one of Rothenburg's puppet shows at **Am Burgtor** to attending a cabaret performance in Munich's traditional **Drehleier** (Rosenheimerstrasse 123, tel: 089-482742) to simply drinking late into the night at a beer hall or village *Volksfest* and engaging in conversation with the locals.

The **Kinocenter Garmisch and Aspentheater im Lamm** (Marienplatz, tel: 08821-2470) in Garmisch-Partenkirchen is a pleasant cinema which screens current English-language films; both Munich's **Cinema** (Nymphenburger Strasse 31, tel: 089-555255) and **Museumlichtspiele** (Lilienstrasse 2, tel: 089-482403) also include many English-language films on their extensive programmes. All three sell popcorn.

Calendar of Special Events

Between Catholic holidays and local traditions, Bavaria is without doubt the festival capital of Germany. Its towns host such a wide variety of folk festivals and traditional fairs that there is something going on somewhere almost any time of year.

FEBRUARY/MARCH

11 November, at 11.11am, is the official beginning of Germany's Carnival season, but the real celebrating doesn't start until a few weeks before **Faschingsdienstag** (Shrove Tuesday, or Mardi Gras). On the Tuesday itself, Bavaria takes half a day off, and towns fill with crowds of costumed revellers anxious to squeeze in a last bit of excess before the rigours of Lent close in. For this fasting season, Bavarian monks brewed their beer extra-strong to compensate for the pangs of hunger. Hence Munich's **Strong Beer Festival** (*Starkbierfest*) in early March at the Salvatorkeller am Nockherberg, where people get down to some serious drinking.

Knights at Kaltenberg

MAY/JUNE

The Thursday after Trinity Sunday which usually falls in early June, i **Fronleichnam**, Corpus Christi. Street are lined with green tree branches and processions of priests and singer bear banners and holy images throug town. Near Füssen, on the lak Forggensee, the procession is born across the water on boats.

Every fourth year, at the end o June, the city of Landshut celebrate its Wedding. Not just any wedding but the marriage of George, Duk Ludwig the Rich's eldest son, whic took place in 1475. Regarded as im pressively excessive at the time, th Wedding is re-enacted in the cours of a three-week folk festival. The ne **Landshuter Hochzeit** will be held i 2001.

Held every tenth year from May t September is the **Passion Play** at Obe ammergau, a day-long performance r enacting the life of Christ. The ne performance is scheduled for the yea 2000.

JULY/AUGUST

avarian villages herald the lazy days
summer with special festivals of their
vn. In Franconia, nearly every week-
d sees a **wine festival** (*Weinfest*). A
ajor Franconian folk festival is the
iliani in Würzburg, held the first
vo weeks of July.

In Lower Bavaria, beer is drunk at
llage folk festivals; one such fair is
raubing's popular *Gäubodenfest* in
ugust. Every five years the Upper
avarian town of Mittenwald returns
its roots with the medieval Bozener
arkt, held in the last two weeks of
ly. Equally old-fashioned, but more
ergetic, is the **Kaltenberger Ritter-
rnier**, a medieval tournament in a
llage just north of Ammersee, also
ld in July.

On the Romantic Road, Dinkels-
hl has a special July festival, too.
1632, so it's said, children saved the
wn by running out in front of the
vedish army and begging for mercy.
day, the **Dinkelsbühler Kinderzeche**
commemorated with a cheerful ten-
y festival, around the third Mon-
y in July.

SEPTEMBER/OCTOBER

ery autumn, the cows which have
azed all summer in the Alps are
orned with flowers and driven back
rough the village streets to their
rns for the winter. This custom, the
babtrieb, is an excuse for much fes-
ity in Upper Bavarian towns, par-
ularly Garmisch, in late September
early October.

September also sees the beginning of
unich's **Oktoberfest**, which runs for
o weeks and three weekends, ending
e first weekend in October. The
eresienwiese, the site on which the
nt is held, is converted into a small
y visited by some 8 million people.

But the fairground is a sideshow to
the main purpose of the festivities,
namely the consumption of beer which
takes place in massive tents set up by
the city's six brewers.

NOVEMBER

St Leonard's Day falls on 6 November. The patron saint of animals is
honoured by farmers who hang his
picture on stable doors and along
Alpine paths. The custom of having
one's horses blessed and then riding
around the town church, **Leonardiritt**,
has developed into a festival in Bad
Tölz, Benediktbeuren and other Upper
Bavarian towns.

DECEMBER

In early December little wooden huts
spring up in the main squares of cities
and towns, selling Christmas ornaments, local crafts, and hot mulled
wine (*Glühwein*). Most famous of these
Christmas markets is the original one
in Nuremberg, renowned for its gin-
gerbread (*Lebkuchen*).

On 6 December, you may run into
St Nicholas himself, distributing gifts
to the children, accompanied by *Kram-
pus*, who carries soot for naughty boys
and girls.

As his day falls on 31 December,
St **Sylvester** has given his name to the
German New Year's Eve, celebrated
everywhere with plenty of fireworks
and plenty of champagne.

PRACTICAL information

GETTING THERE

By Air

Opened in May 1992, the new Munich airport offers services to most worldwide destinations. When you arrive, follow signs to the green S for S-Bahn, the train to the city centre. The journey takes about forty minutes, about the same time as a taxi; but bear in mind that a taxi can cost around DM100. There's also a Lufthansa airport bus that runs regularly to and from the Hauptbahnhof (DM15 one way).

TRAVEL ESSENTIALS

When to Visit

If I were planning a trip to Bavaria, I'd go in May, August to October, or December. In May, you risk spring showers – but you always risk showers when you travel in Central Europe, and you're rewarded with the sight of blossoming apple trees and forsythia on the green hills. Late summer, the one time when the region can be pretty much counted on to be warm, means lounging in beer gardens, boating on the lakes or hiking in the mountains.

September puts a nip in the air and turns everything in the country gold, with a blue-and-white sky the colours of the diamonds on the Bavarian flag. And while the weather in December may be cold, the

Munich airpo

snow brings ski season; while the illum nated wooden stalls of *Christkindl* marke transform cities and towns into pictur postcard holiday fantasies.

Weather

The only thing you can be sure of abo Bavarian weather – indeed, about Ce tral European weather in general – is th it may well rain, especially in any mon that isn't July or August. You can al expect it to be grey, and sometimes fierce cold, in winter. Not to say that there aren many warm, sunny days between Ap and October; and summers seem to be ge ting increasingly hot.

Despite its lakes, Bavaria is a landlock region, and anyone coming from a hum climate will notice how dry it is. Anoth peculiarity is the wind called *Föhn*. A r sult of climatic conditions created by t

ountains, the wind, which causes headaches
nd mood swings (in fact, the *Föhn* defence
vill stand up in court), is likely to be
lowing on sunny, crystal-clear days, when
he mountains seem close enough to touch.
t's particularly noticeable if you're in a
ar; drivers seem to go crazy on *Föhn* days.

The altitude also makes people very sen-
tive to their circulatory systems; *Kreis-
aufstörungen* (circulatory disorders) are
common ailment. The traditional treat-
ent is a glass of champagne; the bub-
les, it seems, are very good indeed for
our circulation.

Clothing

Vhatever the season, make sure you pack
few warm clothes, a sweater or jacket,
nd, in winter, a warm coat. If you're ar-
iving in summer, however, you'll need
ome real hot-weather garb – and don't
rget to bring a bathing suit in case you
ant to dip into a mountain lake or one
f the clean, park-like public pools. Good
alking shoes are vital.

Electricity

avarian outlets have standard European
oltage: 220v. If you're coming from the
K, you'll need a plug adaptor before
our appliance will work with a German
cket; Americans need AC adaptors, as
ell, to convert the voltage.

Time Differences

ll of Germany is in the same, Central
uropean time zone, which means that
's one hour later in Germany than it is
Great Britain, six hours later than it
in Boston, and nine hours later than
eattle.

GETTING ACQUAINTED

Geography

avaria is the southernmost state of Ger-
any, bordering on Austria to the south
nd the Czech Republic to the east. Its
tire southern border is drawn along the
lps; another mountainous region is the
nge running through the Bavarian For-
t, the Upper Palatinate Forest, and
e Fichtel Mountains, bordering on the
zech Republic.

Traditionally, Bavaria's northern border was formed by the River Danube
(*Donau*); today, the state extends much
farther north. The Danube is only one of
several major rivers that have formed trade
routes from time immemorial, including
the Isar, Inn, and Lech flowing up into
it from the south, and the Main in Franconia (a canal linking the Main with the
Danube was opened in late 1992, com-
pleting a route of waterways reaching from
the North Sea to the Black Sea). Bavaria
– particularly Upper Bavaria – is also famous for its many beautiful lakes.

Government and Economy

The Free State of Bavaria is the largest
of the 16 German states, and is, like them,
represented in both the Parliament and
the Senate (*Bundestag* and *Bundesrat*) of
the Federal Government. It is, however,
the only German state to have its own
Senat as well as the usual State Parliament (*Landtag*). Below these in authority
are the governments of the seven provinces
which comprise the state.

Since the war, Bavaria has traditionally been arch-conservative, with its own
majority political party, the CSU, which
is even farther right than the conservative party of the rest of Germany, the CDU.
The CSU was led for years by Franz-Josef
Strauss, whose 'reign' ended with his death
in 1988; since then, his party has lost
quite a bit of its popular support. One of
Bavaria's ironies is that this conservative
bastion is governed from the city of Munich, where the party in power is the left-
wing SPD, in a coalition with the Green
Party.

Traditionally agricultural, and still Germany's leading food producer, Bavaria has
become increasingly important as a cen-

tre for science and big business since the war. Although the farmhouses and grazing cattle aren't likely to vanish from the landscape, they've had to make room for edifices like the huge BMW plant in Dingolfing. Siemens, it's said, has employed one out of every ten Bavarians at some point in its history. And, with the arrival of computer companies from home and abroad on the scene, the area around Munich is known as 'Germany's Silicon Valley'. Munich is a favourite site for trade fairs and expositions, making it a focal point for industries from fashion, watches and jewellery to computers and cars.

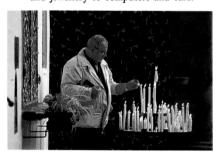

Religion

Asked to describe his countrymen in an English-language assignment for school, a child I know wrote, 'The Bavarians are short and dark, and they are Catholic'. Whether or not it's because of the heritage of the *Baiuvarii* tribe which settled here after the Romans left, it's true that Bavarians tend to possess the dark complexions typical of natives of more southern climes.

As far as religion is concerned, although Protestantism came into some parts of Franconia in the 16th century, the region continues to be predominantly Catholic – a fact most noticeable from the many public and bank holidays, such as Corpus Christi or Assumption Day, which can come as a complete surprise to Protestant visitors (or absent-minded residents, for that matter). Catholicism is also evident in the common salutation *Grüß Gott*, God's greeting, which replaces *Guten Tag* (good day) in this part of the German-speaking world (don't use it, however, in Frankfurt or Hamburg, unless you want to be the object of much merriment).

Currency

The basic unit of German currency is a mark (DM), divided into 100 pfennigs. Coins come in 1, 2, 5, 10, and 50 pfennig denominations, as well as 1, 2, and 5 marks; notes start at 10 and go up. New currency was introduced in the late 1980s; the flashy new bills, with such features as a silver strip running through the note or the numbers in Braille, have since served as a model for the banknotes of other countries, such as Croatia.

Credit cards are not widely accepted. If you haven't got Eurocheques, you'll often have to pay *bar* (cash). Nearly every town has an automatic teller which accepts Eurocards, as well, sometimes, as other credit cards. In Munich, near Marienplatz, the Sparkasse has automatic tellers which exchange foreign bills for German currency.

If you're not near such a facility, you'll have to find a *Wechselstube* (currency exchange). In large cities, the railway station often has a bank outlet which is open later than 3.30pm; in Munich, it's open until 10pm.

Tipping

As a service charge is included in restaurant prices, it's customary to show your appreciation for good service simply by rounding up the bill a mark or two when you pay the waiter or waitress. The same rule holds true in taxis. In large hotels, however, international tipping customs still hold.

By Train

German trains are fast, efficient, and expensive. If you're 26 or under, you qualify for youth fares; while if travelling a long distance over a weekend, you may qualify for a special saver's fare (*Sparpreis* or *Supersparpreis*, depending on the distance), a round-trip discount which allows a second person to come along for half price. For short distances, however, there's very little you can do except grin and pay up. If you're resident in Ger-

92

check periodically to make sure everyone is legal; fines are annoyingly steep if you're caught. Most cities offer day tickets which allow unlimited travel after morning rush hour, or family tickets allowing several people to go together.

By Car

Introduced during the 1930s, the German *Autobahn* has achieved something of a legendary status in Europe. If you've always dreamed of being in a Formula One race, you could really enjoy the *Autobahn* experience. There are no speed limits, and you can guarantee you will be passed by a streamlined BMW no matter how fast you're going. If you would prefer to see the countryside at a more leisurely pace, it's advisable to take the regular *Bundesstrassen* (B).

any, you can buy a Bahn Card, which entitles you to one year of half-price travel nd costs DM220.

Special train lines are added vacation attractions in certain areas, such as the funicular train from Garmisch up the ugspitze; the steam locomotive that operates through Franconia's 'Little Switzerland'; and the locomotive that carries assengers to and from the ferry dock at hiemsee.

AYERISCHE ZUGSPITZBAHN
lympiastrasse 27, Garmisch
el: 08821-7970
esponsible for funicular trains and cable cars up the Zugspitze. English brochure vailable.

RANCONIAN SWITZERLAND STEAM TRAIN
(Dampfbahn Fränkische Schweiz)
ostfach 1, 91320 Ebermannstadt
el: 09131-65873
unday service between Forchheim/ eringersmühle and Ebermannstadt on vinge trains from the 1930s, May–eptember.

HIEMSEE-BAHN
estrasse 108, Prien
l: 08051-6090
entury-old rail service from Prien to the rry dock at Stock (2km).

Bus, Tram, Underground

erman public transport works on an honrs system, which often seems more comicated than need be. Tickets are available om vendors sporting a 'K' over their osks, or from automats in underground ations and even on trams. After you buy ticket, you have to cancel it in a small achine marked with an 'E'. Conductors

One way of getting around

HOURS & HOLIDAYS

Business Hours

In Germany, business hours are strictly controlled. Shops are generally open from 8 or 9am to 6pm; in smaller towns or less central neighbourhoods, they often close for lunch. On Saturdays, they close at 1 or 2pm, except for the first Saturday of the month, *langer Samstag*, when stores in town centres are open until 4pm. Recently instituted, amid much discussion, is 'long Thursday', *langer Donnerstag*, when many establishments stay open until 8.30pm, and even banks, which normally close at 3.30pm, are open until 5.30pm. On Sundays, all you'll find open are bakeries which double as cafés and shops at petrol stations, railway stations or airports which charge exorbitant prices.

Public Holidays

Bavaria has so many public holidays it's hard to keep track of them. This is a partial listing:
New Year's Day
Epiphany (*Heilige Drei Könige*)
Shrove Tuesday (*Faschingsdienstag*)
  (shops close at noon)
Good Friday (*Karfreitag*)
Easter Monday
Ascension Day (*Christi Himmelfahrt*)
Whit Monday (*Pfingstmontag*)
Corpus Christi (*Fronleichnam*)
Assumption Day (*Maria Himmelfahrt*)
German Unity Day 3 October
Christmas Eve (*Heiliger Abend*)
First and Second Christmas Days
(*1. und 2. Weihnachtstag*)

ACCOMMODATION

In the summer months, it can be very difficult to find a hotel room in the Alpine regions of Bavaria. Virtually every farmhouse, however, offers rooms for rent (*Zimmer, Fremdenzimmer*), and often these accommodations are as pleasant and comfortable as any you'll find – and cheaper than some.

In the listing below, approximate prices for a double room are given as $ = DM100–150; $$ = DM150–200; $$$ = DM200+.

Munich

The season you should avoid, or book months in advance, is Oktoberfest in Munich (the last two weeks in September, through early October). There's not a hotel bed to be had.

All the international hotel chains are represented in Munich. Here is a small selection of more intimate establishments, all recommended for their comfort and convenience.

HOTEL LEOPOLD
Leopoldstrasse 119, 80804 Munich
Tel: 089-367061
Situated in northern Schwabing, a mere five-minute walk from Münchner Freiheit, this small hotel, despite its position on

Flower arrangements in Rothenburg

busy Leopoldstrasse, is comfortable, conveniently located, and benefits from an in-house restaurant. $$

DOLLMANN AM MAXMONUMENT
Thierschstrasse 49, Munich
Tel: 089-238080
A comfortable, elegant but not stuffy hotel in a great central location, the residential area of Lehel, a short walk from Maximilianstrasse. $$–$$$

PENSION FRANK
Schellingstrasse 24, 80799 Munich
Tel: 089-281451
In the heart of Schwabing, this pension is renowned as the place where models stay when in Munich for photo shoots. $/$$

HOTEL KÖNIGSWACHE
Steinheilstrasse 7, 80333 Munich
Tel: 089-5427570
A clean, mid-priced hotel located a short walk from the museums, near the Technical University, with a Chinese restaurant on the ground floor. $$

The Alps (Upper Bavaria)
Füssen and Environs

ZUM HECHTEN
Ritterstrasse 6, 87629 Füssen
Tel: 08362-7906 or 6801
In the old city centre, not far from the river, a pleasant establishment complete with restaurant. $

A typical Gaststätte in Upper Bavaria

OTEL ALPENSCHLÖSSLE
atseestrasse 28, 8958 Füssen (Bad ulenbach)
l: 08362-4017
easant surroundings and fine dining. *$$*

Garmisch/Grainau

BSEE HOTEL
491 Grainau-Eibsee
l: 08821-98810
luxurious hotel with a wonderful view.
you're up for an Alpine splurge, this
the place. *$$$*

Mittenwald

OTEL ALPENROSE
ermarkt 1, 82481 Mittenwald
l: 08823-5055
old Bavarian establishment at the heart
town. *$$*

ST-HOTEL
ermarkt 9, 82481 Mittenwald
l: 08823-1094
so central, but outfitted with more lux-
ous trappings such as sauna, solarium,
. *$$*

Berchtesgaden and Environs

PENHOTEL KRONPRINZ
Brandholz,
471 Berchtesgaden
: 08652-6070
short walk from the centre, near the
lway station, this comfortable hotel of-
s luxuries (sauna etc), a restaurant (din-
only), and a mountain view. *$$*

TEL-GASTHOF NUTZKASER
Gseng 10, 83486 Ramsau
: 08657-388 or 619
ountry hotel with panoramic view and
d, cheap restaurant. *$*

Romantic Road
Augsburg

TEL ULRICH
uzinergasse 6, 86150 Augsburg
0821-34610
off of Maximilianstr., this hotel is
r enough to be within an easy walk
ights and nightlife, but located on a
et narrow street. *$$*

Dinkelsbühl

WEISSES ROSS
Steingasse 12, 91550 Dinkelsbühl
Tel: 09851-2274
A renovated stable, with rooms furnished
in a modern Bavarian style, forms the sec-
ond of this hotel's two buildings. *$$*

Rothenburg

BURG HOTEL
*Klostergasse 1–3, 91541 Rothenburg ob
der Tauber*
Tel: 09861-5037
You can't beat the romance of this ivy-
covered hotel with individually-furnished
rooms and suites, each with a view out
over the Tauber valley. *$$$*

Würzburg

HOTEL REBSTOCK
Neubaustrasse 7, 97070 Würzburg
Tel: 0931-30930
Elegant, glossy, and in the heart of down-
town, with a renowned restaurant. *$$$*

Franconia
Bamberg

BRUDERMÜHLE
Schranne 1, 96049 Bamberg
Tel: 0951-955220
A pleasant hotel in the heart of the old
city. *$$*

ST NEPOMUK UND GÄSTEHÄUSER
Obere Mühlbrücke 9, 96049 Bamberg
Tel: 0951-98420
Right on the river. *$$$*

Bayreuth

ZUR LOHMÜHLE
Badstrasse 37, 95444 Bayreuth
Tel: 0921-53060

Nice little hotel with restaurant, both bordering on the stream powering the mill for which the place is named. *$$*

Pegnitz

PFLAUMS POSTHOTEL PEGNITZ
Nürnbergerstrasse 12–16, 91257 Pegnitz
Tel: 09241-7250
The preferred accommodation for Bayreuth Festival-goers. *$$$*

Nuremberg

HOTEL FACKELMANN
Essenweinstrasse 10, 90443 Nürnberg
Tel: 0911-206840
A short walk from the city centre, near the railway station, in a modern part of the city. *$$*

HAUS AM SCHÖNEN BRUNNEN
Hauptmarkt 17, 90403 Nürnberg
Tel: 0911-224225
Excellent location right on the main square. Reserve in advance for *Christkindlmarkt*. *$–$$*

Niederbayern/Lower Bavaria
Passau

HOTEL WILDER MANN
Am Rathausplatz, 94032 Passau
Tel: 0851-35071
One of Passau's oldest hotels, containing the Glass Museum. *$$*

HOTEL ZUM KÖNIG
Rindermarkt 2, 94032 Passau
Tel: 0851-34098
The yellow-and-white baroque facade alone is worth the price of a room – which is surprisingly low. *$*

Sign of hospitality

Regensburg and Environs

BISCHOFSHOF
Krauterermarkt 3, 93047 Regensburg
Tel: 0941-59086
Just behind the Cathedral, this comfortable yet affordable hotel has a number different (and reputable) restaurants of fering everything from fine dining (try t Danube fish) to rustic Bavarian charm as well as an in-house brand of beer. *$*

HOTEL KRIEGER
Mariaort, 93186 Regensburg
Tel: 0941-80018
In a lovely location on the banks of t Naab river, 10km (6 miles) from Reger burg, with plenty of countryside wal this is a family-run hotel with a distinc Bavarian flavour. *$*

Landshut

HOTEL GOLDENE SONNE
Neustadt 520, 84028 Landshut
Tel: 0871-92530
An old-timey *Gasthof* in operation sir 1400, complete with restaurant and own beer garden. *$$*

COMMUNICATIONS & MEDIA

Dialling internationally is straightforwa The international code from Germany 00. After this, dial the country code: A tralia (61); Italy (39); Japan (81); Netherlands (31); Spain (34); United Ki dom (44); United States and Canada (Long-distance calls can be made from Post Office, which saves you having pay the higher charges levied by hote If using a US phone credit card, dial company's access number: AT&T, 1 0130-0010; MCI, Tel: 0130-0012; Spri Tel: 0130-0013.

Voice of America transmits English-l guage programmes, as does the BBC Wo Service. An Austrian station called B Danube Radio features oldies and big-ba

The early evening news

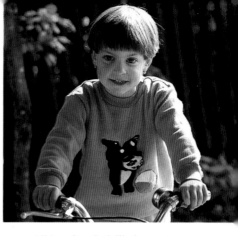

usic. The television station DSF broadasts American football, from the States, a season; while the ABC news and David etterman are broadcast around 1am on TL. The cable stations CNN and Skyhannel (NBC) are available in most big otels.

In Munich, the English-language magzine *Munich Found*, available at many iosks and at the train stations, contains iformation about the city and surunding area, as well as a variety of inresting articles and activity suggestions.

USEFUL INFORMATION

Disabled Facilities

he well-organised system of tourist inrmation offices (*Fremdenverkehrsämter*) roughout Bavaria makes it fairly easy to t information about handicapped facils in the various cities. Augsburg, for ample, has prepared an entire brochure tiled *Leben in der Gemeinschaft* (Livg in the Community), filled with useful dresses and phone numbers of everying from doctors to hotels to public ones which are accessible by wheelchair. While wheelchair users will have fficulty using city buses and trams, the derground in Munich has been steadily stalling more and more lifts, making tually every stop accessible to the handapped. Public buildings erected in rent years, such as the Gasteig Culture ntre, also tend to be fully equipped with ilets and phones for the handicapped; der buildings, such as museums and liaries, are being fitted out with access mps and lifts.

For Children

varia is filled with wonderful things to with children, from boat excursions the Danube to a visit to the Bavaria m Studio in Munich (089-64990), which ers the German version of a Hollywood dio tour. Rothenburg ob der Tauber d Nuremberg both have Doll and Toy useums (in Rothenburg at Hofbronnensse 13. Tel: 09861/7330; in Nuremberg Karlstr. 13–15, tel: 0911-2313164). In nkelsbühl, the small Museum of the ird Dimension presents simple, hands-

on exhibits of optical illusions, stereoscopic slides, and the like (Nördlinger Tor/Stadtmühle, Tel: 09851-6336).

To do justice to Munich's Deutsches Museum (address see *Museums*) can take days: but the coal mine is a hit amongst the children. The same goes for the salt mine in Berchtesgaden.

If you are looking for performances suitable for children, Germany is the right place to be: the major orchestras often give children's concerts, which generally involve some explanation and some audience participation as well as a child-oriented musical or theatre programme. It has been my experience that even children with no German at all enjoy these a great deal. One ambitious Munich Philharmonic soloist arranged a performance of Prokofiev's *Peter and the Wolf* for which the entire audience of children were provided with kazoos; the result was a kind of international communication that left everyone over the age of 12 with a major headache.

A full listing of all such concerts in English can be found in the calendar section of Munich's monthly English-language magazine, *Munich Found*.

Museums

Munich

Alte Pinakothek
One of the great European collections of Old Masters, including room after room of masterpieces by Peter Paul Rubens.
Neue Pinakothek
Situated next to the Alte Pinakothek, this museum concentrates on 19th-century European painting.

Lenbachhaus

Built as a residence by the painter Franz Lenbach, this villa contains the seminal collection of works by the Expressionist *Blaue Reiter* school (including Kandinsky, and Marc), and also presents modern exhibitions.

Münchner Stadtmuseum

City history, from the wooden Moorish dancers to the photography museum, as well as rotating exhibitions, and a film museum.

Deutsches Museum

The world's largest museum of science and technology with hands-on exhibits about everything from coal mining to astronomy. The 'Forum of Technology' contains Germany's first IMAX cinema.

Glyptothek

Ancient Greek and Roman sculpture.

Haus der Kunst

One wing houses a modern art collection, but the main draw are major rotating exhibitions.

BMW Museum

In a futuristic building near the Olympic Park. A fascinating look at the development of the ultimate driving machine.

Villa Stuck

The former home of eccentric artist Franz von Stuck offers Art Nouveau-style rooms and changing exhibitions.

Füssen

Museum of the City of Füssen
Exhibitions on the city's history include a description of the craft of lute-making.

Garmisch

Freilichtmuseum an der Glenleiten
Amerang (Kochel/Murnau exit from A95/Garmisch Autobahn). Open year round. This is the largest open-air museum in Bavaria and consists of a selec-

tion of authentic buildings moved her from different regions, designed to show traditional rural lifestyles and architecture

Among the main attractions are a water mill and a blacksmith's.

Mittenwald

Museum of Violin-Making
Instruments and documents pertaining t the town's traditional craft.

Berchtesgaden

Schloss Museum
From wooden sculptures to city histor to the furnished rooms of the Wittel bach's summer palace, it's all here in th Romanesque or baroque rooms of this ram bling palace.

Augsburg

Staatsgalerie in the Schaezler Palace
Wonderful painting collection in a baroqu residential palace.

Roman Museum
Relics from the first heyday of this forme Roman capital, located in an old Domin can church.

Swabian Crafts Museum (*Handwerk Museum*)
Traditional local crafts, complementir the *Handwerker Route* through the ci where you can see craftsmen still practi ing their trades.

Rothenburg

Museum of Crime
From medieval stocks to the infamous Irc Maiden, a comprehensive history of m dieval punishment. Exhibits explained English.

Imperial City Museum
This museum, located in a 13th-centu Dominican monastery, exhibits about t city's history from the Stone Age to t present.

Inside the Glenleiten museum

Würzburg

ainfränkisches Museum
cated in the baroque *Zeughaus* on
arienburg, this museum has a fantastic
lection of Franconian art and cultural
jects.

Bamberg

ocesan Museum
easures from the religious history of the
y, from Byzantine fabrics and hangings
baroque.
story Museum
ltural and art history of the region
ound Bamberg.
anconian Brewing Museum
ms historically used for beer produc-
n, suitably displayed in an old
nastery brewery.
rl May Museum
e home of the popular author whose
oks have been loved by generations of
ung Germans.

Bayreuth

us Wahnfried
hard Wagner's home is a museum ded-
ted to him, complete with scores and
er memorabilia.

Tüchersfeld

anconian Switzerland Museum
(*änkische Schweiz Museum*)
ibits about geology, regional living,
l Jewish culture, located in an 18th-
tury complex of Jewish buildings.

Nuremberg

manisches Nationalmuseum
unded in the 19th century, this is a
seum for all of Germany with paint-
and sculpture, toys and textiles, and
man history from prehistoric times to
present.
nsport Museum (*Verkehrsmuseum*)
ook at the history of transport, in the
that saw the first German railroad in
5.

Zwiesel

est Museum (*Waldmuseum Zwiesel*)
ibits about the Bavarian Forest,
esel glass and local traditions and
tyles.

Glass Museum
Glass creations old and new.

Tittling/Bavarian Forest

Farmer's Museum (open-air)
One of the best of Bavaria's open-air museums, where various old farm buildings
and dwellings have been moved from all
over the region to give a flavour of daily
life in the past.

Classical forms in Munich's Glyptothek

Passau

Museum in the Veste Oberhaus
In the hilltop castle, Passau cultural his-
tory and an observation tower.
Roman Museum/Boiotro Castle
Prehistory and archaeology, as well as ex-
cavations of Roman ruins.
Passau Glass Museum
More than 30,000 objects document 200
years of glass-making history. Located in
the hotel Wilder Mann.

Regensburg

Castle Museum (*Schlossmuseum*)
Former monastery building redone in the
19th century as the sumptuous palace of
the Counts of Thurn und Taxis.
Diocesan Museum St Ulrich
Gothic art treasures displayed in an old
church building.
Museum of the City of Regensburg
History, art and culture of Eastern
Bavaria.

Landshut

**City Museum and City Painting Collec-
tion in the Residence**
In the former, artifacts from prehistoric
times, the Romans, and the Middle Ages;
in the latter, German painters from the
16th–19th centuries.

Hard to speak and even harder to understand, the Bavarian dialect involves a lot of rounded, long vowels and swallowed word endings. In general, negotiations in halting High German (*Hochdeutsch*) are preferable to attempts to master the local argot – unless you've lived in Bavaria for quite a while. But some elements of the following mini-glossary – such as greetings and leave-takings – are 100 percent Bavarian.

Note that the letter which looks like a funny B (ß) is actually a double S (Straße is the same as Strasse). Umlauts over vowels – ä, ö, ü – are the equivalent of placing an E after the vowel (*schön*, beautiful, is the same as *schoen*), and pronounced by pursing your lips as you speak the word. Often, this simply has the effect of Americanising the purer, European vowels – at McDonald's, a favourite meal is the 'Big Mäc'. Nouns, by the way, are always written with capital letters. In some cases, phonetic approximations are given of the terms below.

Greetings and Numbers

Greeting	*Grüß Gott*
Goodbye	*Tschüß*; *Ade*; *Servus* (as well as *Auf Wiedersehen*, high German)
Please	*Bitte* (or *bitte schön*)
Thank you	*Danke* (or *danke schön*)
How much?	*Wieviel* (vee feel)
What time...	*Wieviel Uhr*
Where is...	*Wo ist...*
Left, right	*Links, rechts*
Straight on	*Geradeaus*
City map	*Stadtplan*
Do you have...	*Haben Sie...*
I need...	*Ich brauche...*
I'd like...	*Ich möchte...*
Pay	*Bezahlen*
	(also used to request the bill at a restaurant: *Bezahlen, bitte*)
Receipt	*Quittung*
Single room	*Einzelzimmer*
Double room	*Doppelzimmer*
One night	*Eine Nacht*
Two nights	*zwei Nächte*
Shower	*Dusche* (doo-sha)
Bathroom	*Toilette* (twa-letta), *Klo*, *WC* (vey sey)

Women	*Damen* (dahmen)
Men	*Herren* (hairen)
Children	*Kinder*
Shop	*Geschäft, Laden*
Clothes	*Kleider*
one	*eins*
two	*zwei*
three	*drei*
four	*vier*
five	*fünf*
six	*sechs*
seven	*sieben*
eight	*acht*
nine	*neun*
ten	*zehn*
twenty	*zwanzig*

Food

This listing may help you find what y want on the average menu.

Semmel	roll
Brez'n	pretzel
Knödel	dumpling
Spätzle	small, chewy noodles
Kartoffel	potato
Kraut, Kohl	cabbage
Rosenkohl	Brussels sprouts
Pepperoni	hot green peppers
Zwiebel	onion
Knoblauch	garlic
Schweinsbraten	roast pork
Rinderbraten	roast beef
Kalb	veal
Kalbskopf	calf's head
Ochsenschwanz	oxtail
Hax'n	pork knuckle
Rippchen	ribs
Lüngerl	lungs
Nieren	kidneys
Leber	liver
Zunge	tongue
Schinken	ham
Pute, Truthahn	turkey
Geschnetzeltes	meat in small pieces
Schnitzel	cutlet
Forelle	trout
Gulasch	meat stew
Spiegelei	fried egg
Helles	light (beer)
Dunkles	dark (beer)
Spezi	Coke and orange soda
Apfelschorle	half apple juice, half mineral water

Hiking

you like to walk, Bavaria is a good ace to visit. Nearly every region has a twork of well-marked trails, and tourist fices are happy to hand out free maps interesting routes. In the Alps, you can ten take a cable car ride to the top of eak, then enjoy the beautiful walk back wn. From many of the summits hang-ders and paragliders take the quick way to the valley.

The mountains are also filled with pine huts (*Hütten*) where walkers can y the night (in rough-and-ready sur-ndings), enabling you to go on jaunts several days. Further information is ailable from the **Deutsche Alpenverein** raterinsel 5, 80538 München, tel: 089-4940).

Franconian Switzerland is just one re-n with a programme called 'Hiking thout Luggage' (*Wandern ohne Gepäck*), e- to seven-day walking routes where ur luggage is taken from inn to inn, d is waiting for you at your destina-n at the end of the day (for informa-n, contact the Franconian Switzerland urist Office, address below).

Cycling

cycles can be rented in most towns, some-es from the German Railroad (*Deutsche ndesbahn*) or from private shops. In rmisch, **Ferdi's Werkstatt** (Prome-destrasse 14) rents mountain bikes to anyone ready to tackle the Alps; but it's the more level trails along the rivers that draw cyclists in real numbers. The Danube, the Isar, and the Inn are all lined with cycle paths (*Radwege*) on which you can make trips of several days (cycling, if you've a mind to, all the way to Vienna or even Hungary), alternating with travel on certain designated trains where you can take your bike free of charge. Again, tourist offices are well-stocked with maps and plenty of information: notably Pas-sau (the Danube and Inn routes) and Land-shut (the Isar route).

Boating

Lakes Starnberg, Tegernsee, Ammersee, and Chiemsee are just a few of the larger Bavarian lakes that offer boating, but there are many other small lakes scattered throughout the Alps).

To rent a boat on Chiemsee, whether you want a sailboat (*Segelboot*), rowboat (*Rud-erboot*), or paddle-boat (*Tretboot*), call **Bootsverleih G Schraml** (Harrasser Strasse, tel: 08051-4575) or **Bootsverleih Schwarz** (Seestrasse, tel: 08051-61063). Bavaria's rivers also offer plenty of boat-ing opportunities.

In Franconian Switzerland, the adven-turous can rent a kayak in Dous, near Wiesenttal (tel: 09197-1015) and set off down the river Aufsess. If you would pre-fer something on a bigger scale, try an excursion along the River Danube from Passau or Regensburg (one major com-pany is **Donauschiffahrt Wurm & Köck**,

A popular means of descent

A skier's paradise

tel: 0851-929292). The various cruise companies offer trips ranging from afternoon jaunts along the Danube (taking in such sights as the canyon called Donaudurchbruch) to longer outings to cities as far away as Vienna. Enquire at the East Bavarian Tourist Office about passenger trips along the new Rhine-Main-Danube Canal (see *p 104*).

Skiing

In Upper Bavaria, you're in the heart of ski country. Garmisch is a special ski centre (68 miles of downhill trails, 93 of cross-country), but the mountains are criss-crossed with networks of chair lifts, cable cars, and ski trails of all descriptions. Detailed information about trails, package offers, and the like are readily available from the tourist information centres (especially Garmisch, Mittenwald, Berchtesgaden). There are also legion ski schools, for both cross-country and downhill. Special attraction in Garmisch is the Zugspitzplatt, Germany's only skiable glacier.

Remember, though, that the Alps don't have the only skiing in Bavaria. The Bavarian Forest is full of slopes (again, both downhill and cross-country); Zwiesel, for example, has an active winter season with ski schools and rental facilities, and has even hosted World Cup races.

USEFUL ADDRESSES

German Tourist Offices Abroad

Australia
German National Tourist Office, Lufthansa House, 9th Floor, 143 Macquarie Street, Sydney 2000. Tel: (012) 367 38 90, Fax: (012) 367 38 95

Austria
Deutsche Zentrale für Tourismus (DZT Schubertring 12, A-1010 Wien. Tel: (4 513 27 92, Fax: (43) 513 27 91

Canada
German National Tourist Office, 175 Blo Street East, North Tower, Suite 60 Toronto, Ontario, M4W 3R8. Tel: (41 968 15 70, Fax: (416) 968 19 86

Denmark
Tysk Turist-Information, Vesterbrogade D III, DK-1620 Copenhagen V. Tel: (3 12 70 95, Fax: (33) 14 47 47

France
Office National Allemand du Tourisme, Boulevard de la Madeleine, F-75001 Par Tel: (31) 40 20 01 88, Fax: (31) 42 8 02 17

Hong Kong
German National Tourist Office, c. Lufthansa German Airlines, Landma East, 5th Floor, 12 Ice House Street, Ho Kong. Tel: (052) 846 63 88, Fax: (05 810 06 01

Israel
German National Tourist Office, c Lufthansa German Airlines, 1 Ben-Yehu Street, Tel Aviv. Tel: (023) 65 80 35, Fa (023) 66 05 58

Italy
Ente Nazionale Germanico per il Turism Via Soperga 36, I-20127 Milano. Tel: (2) 26111598, Fax: (39 2) 2891449
Centro del Turismo Via G Negri 1 I-20123 Milano. Tel: (39 2) 877323

Japan
German National Tourist Office, Deutsc Kulturzentrum (OAG-Haus), 7-5- Akasaka, Minato-ku, Tokyo 107. Tel: (0 35 86 03 80, Fax: (013) 35 86 50 79

South Africa
German National Tourist Office, c Lufthansa German Airlines, 22 Girt Road, Parktown, Johannesburg 2000. T (011) 643 16 15.
Fax: (011) 484 27 50

pain

Oficina Nacional Alemana de Turismo, San Augustin 2, Plaza de las Cortes, E-28014 Madrid. Tel: (34 91) 429 35 51, Fax: (34 91) 420 24 50

weden

Tyska Turistbyrån, Birger Jarlsgatan 11, Box 7520, S-10392 Stockholm. Tel: (46 8) 679 50 95, Fax: (46 8) 611 11 23

witzerland

Deutsches Verkehrsbüro, Talstrasse 62, CH-8001 Zürich. Tel: (41 1) 221 13 87, Fax: (41 1) 212 01 75

nited Kingdom

German National Tourist Office, Nightingale House, 65 Curzon Street, London W1Y 7PE. Tel: (0171) 495 39 90, Fax: (0171) 495 61 29

nited States

German National Tourist Offices

Los Angeles: 444 South Flower Street, Suite 2230, Los Angeles CA 90071. Tel: (213) 688 73 32, Fax: (213) 688 75 74

New York: Chanin Building, 122 East 42nd Street, 52nd floor, New York, N.Y. 10168. Tel: (212) 308 33 00, Fax: (212) 308 13 22

Chicago: c/o German American Chamber of Commerce, Chicago IL 60603-5978. Fax: (312) 782 38 91

Tourist Offices in Bavaria

When you're looking for the tourist information centre in a strange town, you generally ask directions to the *Fremdenverkehrsamt*, where you can get general information (*Auskunft*). In towns designated *Kurort*, or health resort, the same office is often called *Kurverwaltung*, spa administration.

The centres are usually stocked with a full complement of maps and brochures, many of them in English; the staff will also book hotel rooms in any given price category if you contact the office in advance of your trip.

Munich

Fremdenverkehrsamt, Sendlingerstrasse 1 (Ruffini House), Rindermarkt, 80313 München. Tel: 089-2330300. Also: Hauptbahnhof (left of the main entrance) and at the airport (tel: 089-97592815). **Landesfremdenverkehrsverband Bayern**, Prinzregentenstrasse 18/IV, 80538 München. Tel: 089-212397-0, Fax: 089-293582 **Fremdenverkehrsverband München Oberbayern**, Bodensee Strasse 113, 81243 München. Tel: 089-8292180, Fax: 089-82921828.

Schwangau

(King Ludwig's castles)
Kurverwaltung Schwangau, Münchner Strasse 2, 87645 Schwangau. Tel: 08362-81980

Füssen

Kurverwaltung Füssen, Postfach 1165, 87617 Füssen. Tel: 08362-93850

Oberammergau

Verkehrs- und Reisebüro, Gemeinde Oberammergau, Eugen-Papst-Strasse 9a, 82487 Oberammergau. Tel: 08822-1021

Garmisch-Partenkirchen

Verkehrsamt der Kurverwaltung, Schnitzschulstrasse 19, 82467 Garmisch-Partenkirchen. Tel: 08821-1806

Mittenwald

Kurverwaltung, Dammkarstrasse 3, 82481Mittenwald. Tel: 08823-33981

Prien/Chiemsee

Kurverwaltung Prien am Chiemsee, Alte Rathausstrasse 11, 83209 Prien am Chiemsee. Tel: 08051-69050

Berchtesgaden

Kurdirektion des Berchtesgadener Landes, Maximilianstrasse 9, 83471 Berchtesgaden. Tel: 08652-9670

Augsburg

Tourist-Information, Bahnhofstrasse 7 (or Rathausplatz), 86150 Augsburg. Tel: 0821-502070

Fremdenverkehrsverband Allgäu/Bayrisch-Schwaben, Fuggerstrasse 9, 86150 Augsburg. Tel: 0821-33335, Fax: 0821-38331

Dinkelsbühl

Tourist-Information, Fremdeverkehrsamt, Marktplatz, 91550 Dinkelsbühl. Tel: 09851-90240

Rothenburg ob der Tauber

Kultur- und Fremdenverkehrsamt, Rathaus, 91541 Rothenburg ob der Tauber. Tel: 09861-40492

Würzburg

Fremdenverkehrsamt, Am Congress Centrum, 97070 Würzburg. Tel: 0931-372335 (Offices also located at Haus zum Falken am Markt, Hauptbahnhof.)

Bamberg

Städtisches Fremdenverkehrsamt, Geyerswörthstrasse 3, 96047 Bamberg. Tel 0951-871161

Bayreuth

Gästedienst des Fremdenverkehrsvereins Luitpoldplatz 9, 95444 Bayreuth. Tel 0921-88588

Franconian Switzerland

Tourismuszentrale Fränkische Schweiz Oberes Tor 1, 91320. Ebermannstadt. Tel 09194-797779

Nuremberg

Congress- und Tourismus-Zentrale Nürnberg, Verkehrsverein Nürnberg, Frauentorgraben 3, 90433 Nürnberg. Te 0911-23360
(Office also located on Hauptmarkt)

Fremdenverkehrsamt Franken, Am Plärrer 14, 90429 Nürnberg. Tel: 0911 264202, Fax: 0911-270547

Zwiesel

Kurverwaltung, Stadtplatz 27, 9422 Zwiesel. Tel: 09922-1308/9623

Bavarian Forest/Eastern Bavaria

Fremdenverkehrsverband Ostbayern Landshuterstrasse 13, 93047 Regensburg Tel: 0941-585390

Regensburg

Tourist-Information Regensburg, Altes Rathaus, 93047 Regensburg. Tel: 094 507 4410

Passau

Fremdenverkehrsverein Passau, Bahnhofstrasse 36, 94032 Passau. Tel: 085 955980

Landshut

Verkehrsverein Landshut, Altstadt 3 (Rathaus), 84028 Landshut. Tel: 087 922050

Consulates

Australia
...odesberger Allee 107, 53175 Bonn. Tel: ...228-81030
Canada
...al 29, 80331 München. Tel: 089-290650
France
...öhlstrasse 5, 81675 München. Tel: 089-...94110
Ireland
...auerkircherstrasse 1a, 81679 München. ...l: 089-985723
Italy
...öhlstrasse 3, 81675 München. Tel: 089-...80030
Japan
...rinzregentenplatz 10, 81675 München. ...l: 089-471043
South Africa
...ndlinger-Tor-Platz 5, 80366 München. ...l: 089-2311630
Spain
...berföhringerstrasse 45, 81925 München. ...l: 089-985027
United Kingdom
...irkleinstrasse 10, 4th floor, 80538 ...ünchen. Tel: 089-211090
United States
...öniginstrasse 5, 80539 München. Tel: ...9-28880

FURTHER READING

Insight Guide: Germany (Apa Publications, 1992)
Insight Pocket Guide: Munich (Apa Publications, 1992)
Success by Lion Feuchtwanger (Carrol & Graf)
Rise and Fall of the Third Reich by William Shirer
The History of Germany by Golo Mann (Penguin)
Day Trips in Germany by Earl Steinbicker
Baroque Art in Central Europe (Pelican History of Art)

Art & Photo Credits

Photography	Marton Radkai and
Page 72B	Heimo Aga
90	Flughafen München GmbH
67, 69T	Fremdenverkehrsamt Regensburg
20, 21, 37T, 42, 53T, 53B, 58B, 59, 60, 61T, 61B, 62T, 63, 68, 69B, 73, 75B, 76T, 76B, 83, 84B	Wolfgang Fritz
5, 6/7, 10/11, 25T, 31B, 58, 66, 72, 75T, 88T, 88B, 89, 105T	Heinz Grosse
23, 28T, 48T, 50B, 55, 56T, 71	Jochen Keute
26, 35B	Kurverwaltung Mittenwald
28B, 32T, 34, 35T, 36, 37B, 38T, 40B, 44T, 47B, 70, 79T, 79B, 82T, 84T, 92, 93B, 94, 95, 96T, 97, 98B	Lyle Lawson
71B	Mago-Luftbild
38B, 56B, 57, 62B, 65, 77	Anne Midgette
39, 40T, 41, 101, 102	Klaus Neumann
87T	Werner Neumeister
16B	Stadtarchiv München
33	Tandy Performing Arts Photography
74	Dieter Vogel
Production Editor	Erich Meyer
Handwriting	V. Barl
Cover Design	Klaus Geisler
Cartography	Berndtson & Berndtson

sight Guides

er every major destination in every continent.

Bhutan★
Boston★
British Columbia★
Brittany★
Brussels★
Budapest &
  Surroundings★
Canton★
Chiang Mai★
Chicago★
Corsica★
Costa Blanca★
Costa Brava★
Costa del
Sol/Marbella★
Costa Rica★
Crete★
Denmark★
Fiji★
Florence★
Florida★
Florida Keys★
French Riviera★
Gran Canaria★
Hawaii★
Hong Kong★
Hungary
Ibiza★
Iceland★
Ireland's Southwest★
Israel★
Istanbul★
Jakarta★
Jamaica★
Kathmandu Bikes &
  Hikes★
Kenya★
Kuala Lumpur★
Lisbon★
Loire Valley★
London★
Macau
Madrid★
Malacca
Maldives
Mallorca★
Malta★
Mexico City★
Miami★
Milan★
Montreal★
Morocco★
Moscow
Munich★

Nepal★
New Delhi
New Orleans★
New York City★
New Zealand★
Northern California★
Oslo/Bergen★
Paris★
Penang★
Phuket★
Prague★
Provence★
Puerto Rico★
Quebec★
Rhodes★
Rome★
Sabah★
St Petersburg★
San Francisco★
Sardinia
Scotland★
Seville★
Seychelles★
Sicily★
Sikkim
Singapore★
Southeast England
Southern California★
Southern Spain★
Sri Lanka★
Sydney★
Tenerife★
Thailand★
Tibet★
Toronto★
Tunisia★
Turkish Coast★
Tuscany★
Venice★
Vienna★
Vietnam★
Yogyakarta
Yucatan Peninsula★

★ = *Insight Pocket*
Guides
with Pull out Maps

Algarve
Amsterdam
Bahamas
Bali
Bangkok

Barbados
Barcelona
Beijing
Belgium
Berlin
Brittany
Brussels
Budapest
Burgundy
Copenhagen
Costa Brava
Costa Rica
Crete
Cyprus
Czech Republic
Denmark
Dominican Republic
Dublin
Egypt
Finland
Florence
Gran Canaria
Greece
Holland
Hong Kong
Ireland
Israel
Italian Lakes
Italian Riviera
Jamaica
Jerusalem
Lisbon
Madeira
Mallorca
Malta
Milan
Moscow
Munich
Normandy
Norway
Paris
Poland
Portugal
Prague
Provence
Rhodes
Rome
St Petersburg
Salzburg
Singapore
Switzerland
Sydney
Tenerife
Thailand

Turkey
Turkish Coast
Tuscany
UK regional titles:
  Bath & Surroundings
  Cambridge & East
    Anglia
  Cornwall
  Cotswolds
  Devon & Exmoor
  Edinburgh
  Lake District
  London
  New Forest
  North York Moors
  Northumbria
  Oxford
  Peak District
  Scotland
  Scottish Highlands
  Shakespeare Country
  Snowdonia
  South Downs
  York
  Yorkshire Dales
USA regional titles:
  Boston
  Cape Cod
  Chicago
  Florida
  Florida Keys
  Hawaii: Maui
  Hawaii: Oahu
  Las Vegas
  Los Angeles
  Martha's Vineyard &
    Nantucket
  New York
  San Francisco
  Washington D.C.
Venice
Vienna
West of Ireland